Agricultural Digitization and Zhongyong Philosophy

This interdisciplinary book combines digital technology with Eastern philosophy to examine how the concept of Zhongyong in Confucianism can be used to coordinate digital technology with sustainable agriculture.

Zhongyong comes from the connotation of moderate and sustainable in ancient Chinese culture. It is with this concept in mind that this book presents a novel collaboration between philosophy and computer technology to explain how Zhongyong can play an important part in realizing agricultural digitization within a circular economy in order to help solve the current food crisis. The book examines two popular, yet contradictory, digital technologies—blockchain and the green data center. It showcases how the use of traditional Chinese Zhongyong can promote the decentralization of blockchain and the centralization of the green data center and explains the advantages of using both technologies simultaneously. The book puts forward a digital circular agricultural framework that embeds both blockchain and the green data center through an actual case study. While this book specifically focuses on agriculture, it also provides readers with a new perspective for thinking further on how to break down the disciplinary barriers between the social sciences and natural sciences.

This book will be of great interest to students and scholars of agriculture, digital technologies, circular economy, sustainable development, and Eastern philosophy.

Yiyan Chen is a full-time PhD candidate in the School of Social Sciences at the Universiti Sains Malaysia. He is also a senior engineer in computer science and a senior economic engineer in business administration.

Hooi Hooi Lean is a professor of Economics in the School of Social Sciences at the Universiti Sains Malaysia. She received Malaysia's Research Star Award in 2017 from the Ministry of Higher Education Malaysia and Clarivate Analytics and was listed in Stanford University's World's Top 2% Scientists.

Ye Li is an assistant professor in the College of Economic and Social Development at Nankai University, Tianjin, China.

Routledge Focus on Environment and Sustainability

For more information about this series, please visit: www.routledge.com/Routledge-Focus-on-Environment-and-Sustainability/book-series/RFES

Agricultural Digitization and Zhongyong Philosophy

Creating a Sustainable Circular Economy

Yiyan Chen, Hooi Hooi Lean, and Ye Li

Routledge
Taylor & Francis Group
LONDON AND NEW YORK

earthscan
from Routledge

First published 2023
by Routledge
4 Park Square, Milton Park, Abingdon, Oxon OX14 4RN

and by Routledge
605 Third Avenue, New York, NY 10158

Routledge is an imprint of the Taylor & Francis Group, an informa business

British Library Cataloguing-in-Publication Data
A catalogue record for this book is available from the British Library

ISBN: 978-1-032-43969-3 (hbk)
ISBN: 978-1-032-43973-0 (pbk)
ISBN: 978-1-003-36966-0 (ebk)

DOI: 10.4324/9781003369660

Typeset in Times New Roman
by Newgen Publishing UK

Contents

Abbreviations

AI	artificial intelligence
APP	application
C/S	client/server
CPU	central processing unit
DAG	directed acyclic graph
DBFT	delegated Byzantine fault tolerant
DCIM	data center infrastructure management
DCN	data center network
DL	distributed ledger
DMaaS	data center management as a service
DTs	digital technologies
EVM	embedded virtual machine
FAO	Food and Agriculture Organization of the United Nations
GAIN	Global Agricultural Information Network
GLCC	green low-carbon coin
GPS	global positioning system
GPT	general purpose technology
GPTs	general purpose technologies
ICT	information and communication technology
IoT	internet of things
IT	information technology
KWH	kilowatt-hours
MD	message digest
MW	megawatt
MySQL	my structured query language

NoSQL	not only structured query language
OSI	open system interconnection
P2P	peer-to-peer
PBFT	practical Byzantine fault tolerance
PC	personal computer
PDU	power distribution unit
PH	potential of hydrogen
PoA	proof of activity
PoB	proof of burn
PoL	proof of luck
PoS	proof of sake
PoW	proof of work
SHA	secure hash algorithm
TCP	transmission control protocol
UPS	uninterruptible power supply
USDA	United States Department of Agriculture
VR	virtual reality
WFP	United Nations World Food Programme
WTO	World Trade Organization

1 Agricultural Digitalization and Its Advantages

Human demand for food forms the basis of agricultural activities. Since human beings learned to use tools, the traces of agricultural activities have become forceful evidence to reveal ancient civilization (Mann, 2005). Agricultural activities are one of the important ways to continue human civilization and the key to meet the basic needs of human survival (Heller and Keoelian, 2003). After the industrial revolution, science and technology became one of the important elements of productivity, and gradually formed a modern agricultural system, which led to more prosperous agriculture (Stone, 2011; Wyckhuys et al., 2020; Hammond et al., 2020). In 2017, many scholars thought that world agriculture development was in the best time (O' Keefe, 2017), and would have a bright and resplendent future (FAO, 2017).

"*There are more things in heaven and earth, Horatio, than are dreamt of in your philosophy*". Unfortunately, as Shakespeare said in Hamlet, COVID-19 cast a shadow over the bright future of global agriculture. Due to the impact of COVID-19, the Food and Agriculture Organization of the United Nations (FAO) believes that the world cannot achieve the plan of "Zero Hunger" by 2030. The food security and nutrition of the most vulnerable population groups have further deteriorated (FAO et al., 2020). The United Nations World Food Programme (WFP) believes that due to the impact of COVID-19, the number of people suffering from chronic hunger in the world will increase to 265 million by the end of 2020, and 300,000 people may die of starvation every day (WFP, 2020). Countries have taken measures to deal with the upcoming food crisis: Cambodia, Vietnam, and Myanmar have banned rice exports; Egypt and Honduras have banned nut exports; Russia, Kazakhstan, and Tajikistan have banned wheat exports. These

DOI: 10.4324/9781003369660-1

abnormal trade restrictions even attracted the attention of the World Trade Organization (WTO) (Muangkaew, 2020). Since the COVID-19 pandemic, 80 countries and customs territories have implemented export bans or restrictions (WTO, 2020), which has caused a huge impact on the global agricultural upstream and downstream industrial chain and its subsidiary industries, aggravating food shortage. This food crisis was called the most serious in the world in 50 years, which put at least 25 countries to face the risk of severe famine in 2020 (FAO and WFP, 2020). With a population of 1.4 billion and a great demand for food, whether China can survive the crisis smoothly has become the focus of global attention. Especially after China stops the "zero COVID-19" policy, whether the food issue will become a stumbling block on China's development path is a question worthy of attention.

Although the COVID-19 pandemic has winded down, the food crisis that the pandemic caused has not died down. Thankfully, long before the outbreak of COVID-19, developed countries and some emerging economies had already started trying to digitize their agricultural or food systems. McAfee (2009) believes that digitalization refers to the path driven by digital technology that can bring changes to human society; Tilson et al. (2010) are of the view that digitalization is the application of digital technology to a wide range of social processes and the environment in which digital technology becomes the infrastructure. At present, there is no clear or unified definition to illustrate the specific meaning of digitalization. Terms such as "digital transformation", "digitalization", "digitalization", and "digitization" are often used interchangeably in existing research (Hausberg et al., 2019; Mergel et al., 2019). Likewise, the term "agricultural digitalization" is not clearly or uniformly defined.

According to existing research, agricultural digitalization is characterized by the use of precise digital technology to help farmers make real-time and targeted agricultural decisions (Wolfert et al., 2017; Rose and Chilvers, 2018; Weersink et al., 2018). Digital technologies used in agricultural digitalization include artificial intelligence (AI), drones, sensors, Internet of Things (IOTs), cloud computing, blockchain, and data centers. These digital technologies are mainly used to optimize agricultural production processes (Walter et al., 2017; Kamilaris et al., 2017), agricultural systems (Basso and Antle, 2020), agricultural trade (Jouanjean, 2019), agricultural industry value chains (Poppe et al., 2013; Smith, 2018), and agricultural governance systems (Ehlers et al., 2021). Digitalization of agriculture can sustainably increase food production and is a promising means of addressing food security for a growing world population (Foley et al., 2011; Shepherd et al., 2020). Furthermore, digitalization of agriculture can alleviate the pressure of resource scarcity and effectively combat climate change (Balafoutis et al., 2017), create high-skilled jobs (Rotz et al., 2019a), improve animal welfare (Dawkins, 2016), and foster global agricultural markets (Jouanjean, 2019). These advantages enable digitalization of agriculture to effectively solve the "three food problems" (Lioutas et al., 2021) proposed by Gilman (1917): "How to produce the most food with the least time, money and labor costs?", "How to distributing food to consumers quickly, efficiently, and economically?", and "How can healthy food be prepared and served at low cost?" Therefore, we define agricultural digitalization as the use of digital technology as a boost to increase food production in many links such as production and consumption in the agricultural field, improve the scientificity and rationality of consumption and distribution, increase the sustainability and efficiency of the agricultural system, and a means to bring about change in global agricultural systems.

However, the digitalization of agricultural systems is a new topic, and whether it can help agricultural systems achieve sustainable development is still controversial and uncertain (Klerkx and Rose, 2020). Skeptics believe that digitalization may not bring too many changes to the agricultural system, nor can it establish an ideal resource-saving, low-pollution, and high-efficiency circular economic system, but only puts a layer on the current economic production model. They think that digitization of the agricultural system is only a continuation of the current economic production model (Bronson and Knezevic, 2016). In addition, public concerns about data sovereignty, ownership and privacy, and how to avoid excessive centralization of large agricultural enterprises through digitalization are also worthy of attention (Rotz et al., 2019a). The digitalization of the agricultural system will also lead to large-scale unemployment of low-skilled labor groups (Carolan, 2020), and even bring global agriculture into an extreme situation of "algorithmic governance" (Henman, 2020). The harm to the environment from the greenhouse gases emitted due to a large amount of electricity consumed by the use of these digital technologies is also worth exploring (Leroux, 2020). In addition, there are some obstacles that will affect the implementation of agricultural digitalization, such as high skill threshold, high investment and maintenance costs, unfriendly operation experience, and subjective distrust of "cold machines".

Take green data centers and blockchains as examples. Green data centers have the advantages of low energy consumption and low pollution, while blockchains have the advantages of openness, sharing, and autonomy. However, both also have some disadvantages. For example, the ultra-high computing power of the green data center will increase the trend of "centralization" in the process of continuous strengthening, which in turn will lead to problems such as monopoly, information opacity, and dictatorship. On the other hand, the "decentralization" trend of the blockchain will breed problems such as decreased cohesion and low decision-making efficiency. Taken together, neither technology is perfect, but there is a complex "Zhongyong" relationship between their respective strengths and weaknesses, that is, "complementary advantages, advantages restrain disadvantages, disadvantages offset disadvantages". This "Zhongyong" relationship provides a potential possibility for the combination of the two digital technologies.

References

Balafoutis, A., Beck, B., Fountas, S., et al. 2017. Precision agriculture technologies positively contributing to GHG emissions mitigation, farm productivity and economics. *Sustainability*, 9(8), 1339.

Basso, B., Antle, J. 2020. Digital agriculture to design sustainable agricultural systems. *Nature Sustainability*, 3(4), 254–256.

Bronson, K., Knezevic, I. 2016. Big Data in food and agriculture. *Big Data & Society*, 3(1), Article Number: 2053951716648174.

Carolan, M. 2020. Automated agrifood futures: robotics, labor and the distributive politics of digital agriculture. *The Journal of Peasant Studies*, 47(1), 184–207.

Dawkins, M. S. 2016. Animal welfare and efficient farming: is conflict inevitable? *Animal Production Science*, 57(2), 201–208.

Ehlers, M. H., Huber, R., Finger, R. 2021. Agricultural policy in the era of digitalisation. *Food Policy*, 100, 102019.

Foley, J. A., Ramankutty, N., Brauman, K. A., et al. 2011. Solutions for a cultivated planet. *Nature*, 478(7369), 337–342.

Food and Agriculture Organization of the United Nations (FAO), 2017. The future of food and agriculture—trends and challenges. FAO, www.fao.org/3/a-i6583e.pdf

Food and Agriculture Organization of the United Nations (FAO), International Fund for Agricultural Development (IFAD), United Nations International Children's Emergency Fund (UNICEF), et al., 2020. The state of food security and nutrition in the world 2020—Transforming food systems for affordable healthy diets. FAO, IFAD, UNICEF, and WHO, www.fao.org/3/ca9692en/online/ca9692en.html

Food and Agriculture Organization of the United Nations (FAO), United Nations World Food Programme (WFP), 2020. FAO-WFP early warning analysis of acute food insecurity hotspots. FAO, WFP, www.fao.org/3/cb0258en/CB0258EN.pdf

Gilman, C. P. 1917. The housekeeper and the food problem. *The Annals of the American Academy of Political and Social Science*, 74(1), 123–130.

Hammond, J., Rosenblum, N., Breseman, D., et al., 2020. Towards actionable farm typologies: Scaling adoption of agricultural inputs in Rwanda. *Agricultural System*, 183, Article Number: UNSP 102857.

Hausberg, J. P., Liere-Netheler, K., Packmohr, S., et al. 2019. Research streams on digital transformation from a holistic business perspective: a systematic literature review and citation network analysis. *Journal of Business Economics*, 89(8), 931–963.

Heller, M.C., Keoelian, G.A., 2003. Assessing the sustainability of the US food system: A life cycle perspective. *Agricultural Systems* 76(3), 1007–1041.

Henman, P. 2020. Improving public services using artificial intelligence: Possibilities, pitfalls, governance. *Asia Pacific Journal of Public Administration*, 42(4), 209–221.

Jouanjean, M. A. 2019. Digital opportunities for trade in the agriculture and food sectors. *OECD Food, Agriculture and Fisheries Papers*, No. 122, OECD Publishing, Paris. https://doi.org/10.1787/18156797

Kamilaris, A., Kartakoullis, A., Prenafeta-Boldú, F. X. 2017. A review on the practice of big data analysis in agriculture. *Computers and Electronics in Agriculture*, 143, 23–37.

Klerkx, L., Rose, D, 2020. Dealing with the game-changing technologies of Agriculture 4.0: How do we manage diversity and responsibility in food system transition pathways? *Global Food Security* 24, Article Number: 100347.

Leroux, C. 2020. Reflecting on the carbon footprint of digital technologies in the AgTech and precision agriculture sectors. www.aspexit.com/en/reflecting-on-the-carbon-footprint-of-digital-in-the-agtech-and-precision-agriculture-sectors/

Lioutas, E. D., Charatsari, C., De Rosa, M. 2021. Digitalization of agriculture: A way to solve the food problem or a trolley dilemma? *Technology in Society*, 67, 101744.

Mann, C.C., 2005. Archaeology—Oldest civilization in the Americas revealed. *Science* 307 (5706), 34–35.

McAfee, A. 2009. *Enterprise 2.0: New Collaborative Tools for Your Organization's Toughest Challenges*. Harvard Business Press, Cambridge, MA.

Mergel, I., Edelmann, N., Haug, N. 2019. Defining digital transformation: Results from expert interviews. *Government Information Quarterly*, 36(4), 101385.

Muangkaew, T., 2020. "WTO bans countries from stopping export of food" due to Covid-19. The Nation Thailand, www.nationthailand.com/news/30390580

O'Keefe, M., 2017. Is this the best time ever for agriculture? U.S. Dairy Export Council, https://blog.usdec.org/usdairyexporter/why-this-is-best-time-to-be-in-agriculture-0

Poppe, K. J., Wolfert, S., Verdouw, C., et al. 2013. Information and communication technology as a driver for change in agri-food chains. *EuroChoices*, 12(1), 60–65.

Rose, D. C., Chilvers, J. 2018. Agriculture 4.0: Broadening responsible innovation in an era of smart farming. *Frontiers in Sustainable Food Systems*, 2, 87.

Rotz, S., Duncan, E., Small, M., et al. 2019a. The politics of digital agricultural technologies: a preliminary review. *Sociologia Ruralis*, 59(2), 203–229.

Rotz, S., Gravely, E., Mosby, I., et al. 2019b. Automated pastures and the digital divide: How agricultural technologies are shaping labour and rural communities. *Journal of Rural Studies*, 68, 112–122.

Shepherd, M., Turner, J. A., Small, B., et al. 2020. Priorities for science to overcome hurdles thwarting the full promise of the 'digital agriculture' revolution. *Journal of the Science of Food and Agriculture*, 100(14), 5083–5092.

Smith, M. J. 2018. Getting value from artificial intelligence in agriculture. *Animal Production Science*, 60(1), 46–54.

Stone, G.D., 2011. Contradictions in the last mile: Suicide, culture, and E-Agriculture in rural India. *Science Technology & Human Values* 36 (6), 759–790.

Tilson, D., Lyytinen, K., and Sørensen, C. 2010. Research commentary—Digital infrastructures: The missing IS research agenda. *Information Systems Research*, 21(4), 748–759.

United Nations World Food Programme (WFP), 2020. WFP Chief warns of hunger pandemic as COVID-19 spreads (Statement to UN Security Council). WFP, www.wfp.org/news/wfp-chief-warns-hunger-pandemic-covid-19-spreads-statement-un-security-council

Walter, A., Finger, R., Huber, R., et al. 2017. Smart farming is key to developing sustainable agriculture. *Proceedings of the National Academy of Sciences*, 114(24), 6148–6150.

Weersink, A., Fraser, E., Pannell, D., et al. 2018. Opportunities and challenges for big data in agricultural and environmental analysis. *Annual Review of Resource Economics*, 10(1), 19–37.

Wolfert, S., Ge, L., Verdouw, C., Bogaardt, M. J. 2017. Big data in smart farming—A review. *Agricultural Systems*, 153, 69–80.

World Trade Organization (WTO), 2020. WTO report finds growing number of export restrictions in response to COVID-19 crisis. WTO, www.wto.org/english/news_e/news20_e/rese_23apr20_e.htm

Wyckhuys, K.A.G., Lu, Y.H., Zhou, W.W., et al., 2020. Ecological pest control fortifies agricultural growth in Asia-Pacific economics. *Nature Ecology & Evolution*, DOI:10.1038/s41559-020-01294-y

2 The Concept, Connotation, and Logic of the Zhongyong

Zhongyong, translated into English as "doctrine of the mean in Confucianism" (Du and Dai, 2018) or "golden mean in Confucianism" (Qin, and Wang, 2011), is a distinguished Chinese philosophical thinking proposed by Confucius (Zi, 2016), which focuses on the dual characters of objects (advantages and disadvantages) and the multiple characteristics of different objects. Considering the opposite but not the contradictory logical relationship, it is a relationship of mutual generation and restriction (Zhou et al., 2020). "Zhong" refers to the state or standard that things are in the optimal equilibrium. This optimal equilibrium is moderate or appropriate, and it is not optimal to exceed or insufficient than this state or standard; "Yong" has two connotations. The first is ordinary, that is, continuous daily life; the second is constancy, that is, permanent immutability. "Zhong" and "Yong" make up "Zhongyong". Therefore, in the continuous daily life, the doctrine of "going beyond the limit is as bad as falling short" is abided by, and things can be in the moderate or appropriate optimal equilibrium position to reach the state of Zhongyong (Key Concepts in Chinese Thought and Culture, 2020), as shown in Figure 2.1.

In Figure 2.1, the yellow sphere represents the object, the green part on the left side represents the insufficient state, and the red part on the right side represents the excess state, while the concave slope is composed of the blue polygonal line AB in the middle represents the moderate state. Proposing the hypothesis that there is no loss of energy, the yellow sphere will repeatedly move along the concave slope composed of the blue polygonal line AB, that is,

DOI: 10.4324/9781003369660-2

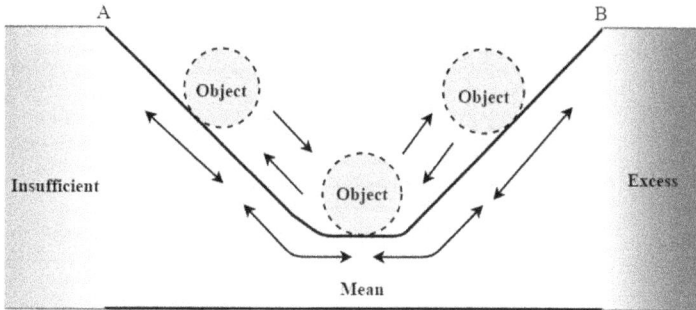

Figure 2.1 Schematic diagram of the state of Zhongyong.

the object will be permanently in a state of dynamic equilibrium in a moderate range.

The Zhongyong was pioneered by Confucius and has been continuously improved by Confucian masters such as Mencius, Yan Hui, Zhu Xi, and Wang Fuzhi. At present, a relatively mature Zhongyong logic system has been formed. Among them, there are the following six common types. Take the two elements of X and Y (or two different aspects of things) as an example:

I The first type is "based on X but also considering Y". This is a more biased logic than "X and Y", that is, "X and Y, and the degree of X is greater than Y". For example, "gong er an" (*a Chinese vocabulary, Chinese phonetic transcription: gōng ér ān*) means solemn but easy-going. Based on "gong" and considering the characteristics of "an", "gong" means solemn and "an" means easy-going, but the degree of "gong" is higher than "an" more. This logic is shown in Figure. 2.2.

II The second type is "both X and Y, and X is as important as Y". There is no priority or degree between X and Y, but a parallel and equal existence. For example, "neng gong neng shou" (*a Chinese idiom, Chinese phonetic transcription: néng gōng néng shǒu*) means that in a war, both the ability to attack the enemy and the ability to defend against the enemy are necessary. "Gong" means the ability to attack the enemy. It is as essential as "shou", which means the ability to defend against the enemy. "gong" and "shou" are equally important. This logic is shown in Figure 2.3.

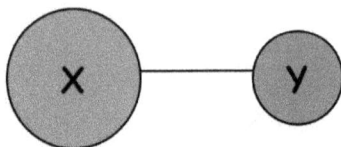

Logic 1: Both X and Y,
and the degree of X is
greater than Y

Figure 2.2 Category I logic of Zhongyong.

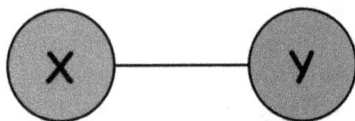

Logic 2: Both X
and Y

Figure 2.3 Category II logic of Zhongyong.

III The third type is "neither X nor Y". This logic is consistent with mathematical logic. According to the concept of the Cantor set, this is the complement of "X or Y", which means that it is neither X nor Y. It is the negation of both elements at the same time. For example, "bu bei bu kang" (*a Chinese idiom, Chinese phonetic transcription: bù bēi bù kàng*) means neither inferiority nor arrogance. "Bei" means inferiority and "kang" means arrogance, and they all express extreme emotions. "Bu" means denial or rejection. "Bu bei" means that person should not be too inferior and "bu kang" means that person should not be too arrogant. This logic is shown in Figure 2.4.

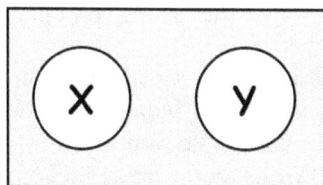

Logic 3: Neither X nor Y, i.e., the yellow part of the universal set

Figure 2.4 Category III logic of Zhongyong.

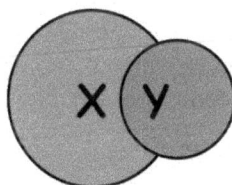

Logic 4: X, yet not extreme X, Y was also taken into account

Figure 2.5 Category IV logic of Zhongyong.

IV The fourth type is "X, yet not extreme X, Y was taken into account also". It means that although things present the state of X, they have not gone to extremes, but also have the nature of Y (Y is usually a concept opposite to X itself or its characteristics), that is, by incorporating some of the properties of Y to neutralize the adverse effects of X and prevent X from going to extremes. For example, "ai er bu shang" (*a Chinese idiom, Chinese phonetic transcription: āi ér bù shāng*) represents the state of feeling sad but not injured by grief. "Ai" means sadness and "shang" means wounded or damaged. From a health perspective, too much "ai" will lead to "shang". "Bu shang" means the denial or rejection of "shang". "Bu shang" can neutralize the "shang" brought by "ai". This logic is shown in Figure 2.5.

V The fifth type is "If not satisfying the condition Z, one of X or Y". It means that only if condition Z exists, X and Y can exist simultaneously. Otherwise, you can only choose one of the two. For example, "yu he xiong zhang bu ke jian de" (*a Chinese idiom, Chinese phonetic transcription: yú hé xióng zhǎng bù kě jiān dé*) means that although "yu" and "xiong zhang" are both delicious food, if your appetite is limited (does not meet the condition Z; condition Z means your appetite is enormous), therefore, you can't eat both "yu" and "xiong zhang". "Yu" means grilled fish or steamed fish and "xiong zhang" means bear paw. They are all delicacies, but you should learn to choose if you don't have the conditions to get them all. You can only select one of the "yu" and "xiong zhang". This logic is shown in Figure 2.6.

VI The sixth type is "X is opposed to Y, only X exists, Y exists, and vice versa". It means that Y can only exist if X exists. If X does not exist, Y does not exist anymore. For example, "dong jing xiang dai" (*a Chinese idiom, Chinese phonetic transcription: dòng*

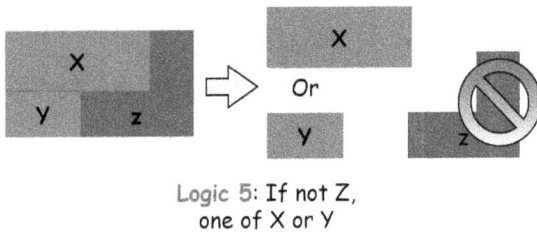

Logic 5: If not Z,
one of X or Y

Figure 2.6 Category V logic of Zhongyong.

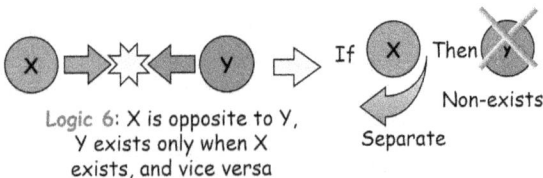

Logic 6: X is opposite to Y,
Y exists only when X
exists, and vice versa

If X Then Y
Non-exists
Separate

Figure 2.7 Category VI logic of Zhongyong.

jìng xiāng dài) means that "dong" and "jing" are interdependent, and they are a pair of relative concepts. "Jing" means quiescency and "dong" means moving. Whether a person in a moving state requires a stationary state to set off, and whether a person in a static state also needs a moving state to set off. "Dong" and "jing" set off each other to create the meaning of their existence. For example, when a supersonic aircraft and a tortoise move simultaneously, the tortoise is as if stationary compared to a supersonic aircraft. If there is no "dong", naturally, there is no so-called jing concept. This logic is shown in Figure 2.7.

The Zhongyong thought is closely bound up with agriculture, and its birth benefited from the cultivation culture in ancient China (He, 2000), which is related to the production and living environment of agrarian society because the circulation of natural phenomena and the natural conditions suitable for farming made the ancient people extremely sensitive to the variation of natural rhythm. For example, the view that "as soon as the sun reaches the meridian it declines", the rainfall distribution, the ebb and flow in the river, the regular changes of the four seasons, and the seasonal solar terms emphasize farming made the ancient Chinese sages pay attention to the interdependence and transformation of objects on the opposite side, thus breeding the Confucian Zhongyong thinking. Zhongyong includes two pivotal thoughts: moderate thinking and comprehensive thinking (Zhou et al., 2019). Moderate thinking opposes objects going to extremes and emphasizes that everything should be presented in a sustainable and non-extreme way. Comprehensive thinking ponders a question from different aspects, that is, in different aspects, the same object will present different evaluations, and to comprehensively judge an object, it's necessary to consider it from different aspects.

Centralization of green data centers and decentralization of blockchain are opposite and interdependent concepts (Blair, 1996; Witesman and Wise, 2009). Both sides have their advantages and disadvantages. Appropriate decentralization and centralization are beneficial (Chen et al., 2020b). In other words, it is not an optimal scheme to implement centralization or decentralization in a system. Therefore, centralization and decentralization coexist, that is, neither complete centralization nor complete centralization is implemented. This approach is in line with the Zhongyong, that is, centralized green data center and decentralized blockchain are both adopted. This combination is called the Zhongyong combination, which is more scientific and reasonable than eclecticism, egalitarianism, and compromise.

Based on these and the above, we believe that it is possible to integrate green data centers and blockchains. This feasibility has laid the foundation for China's traditional philosophical paradigm to guide technology integration, thereby providing circular sustainable development for agriculture and improving the production, consumption, and service links of the agricultural system. We will introduce more details in subsequent chapters.

Therefore, we first demonstrate that green data centers and blockchain are general purpose technologies (GPTs) and have pervasiveness. Then, learning from the Chinese traditional Confucian "Zhongyong" as the logical basis and guiding method for combining the two technologies, this book demonstrates the Zhongyong practicability of the combination of two technologies through the Zhongyong practical method, with the aim of the retaining the technical advantages of both at the same time and complementary, while using the advantages of one side to restrain the disadvantages of another side, and to achieve one side's technical disadvantages to offset another side's disadvantages to the maximum extent. On this basis, taking Beijing Liuminying Ecological Farm as an example, according to its development status and challenges, a "semi-centralized and semi-decentralized" circular agricultural framework based on green data center and blockchain is proposed. This framework can be adopted to improve the agricultural mode of Beijing Liuminying Ecological Farm and provides a path for the ecological farm's development of "digital agriculture". It also acts as a reference for further research on agricultural digitization and its practice in the future.

The main contributions of this book are as follows: (1) By summarizing the existing literature, the advantages and disadvantages of centralization as green data center's inherent technical character and also the advantages and disadvantages of decentralization as blockchain's inherent technical character are analyzed, and the possible impact of "extreme centralization" and "extreme decentralization" on agricultural digital transformation is further discussed; (2) It is demonstrated that green data center and blockchain are both GPTs and have pervasiveness, and reveal the technical logic foundation for the combination of these two technologies; (3) This book introduces the Confucian traditional "Zhongyong" thinking and demonstrates the Zhongyong practicability of the combination between the green data center and blockchain through three necessary conditions of the Zhongyong practical method. It combines philosophical logic with technical logic, which provides a theoretical basis for the Zhongyong combination and Zhongyong practical application of these two advanced technologies; (4) Taking Beijing Liuminying Ecological Farm as an example, according to its current development status and problems, this book proposes a "semi-centralized and semi-decentralized" circular agricultural framework based on green data center and blockchain. This framework contains the Zhongyong philosophical wisdom and can realize "complementary advantages, advantages restrain disadvantages, disadvantages offset disadvantages". Furthermore, it can promote the ecological farm to reform the current circular agricultural mode and realize digital transformation, which will lay a foundation for further discussion on composite applications of green data center and blockchain in the future.

The chapters in this book are as follows: In Chapter 1, we presented the rationale for and benefits of digital transformation in agriculture and explain the feasibility of using digital technology to solve the current food crisis facing agriculture. We put forward the viewpoint of using the idea of the Zhongyong philosophy to integrate the two major digital technologies of the popular blockchain and the green digital center to form a "complementary advantages, advantages restrain disadvantages, disadvantages offset disadvantages" situation. In Chapter 2 (this chapter), we first introduce the definition and connotation of the Zhongyong to readers and then present the six commonly used logics of the Zhongyong to understand this traditional Chinese philosophy. Afterward, the book's research content is summarized logically and the book's innovation, contribution, and chapter arrangement are described. In Chapter 3, we introduce the concept of green data center and its applications in the agricultural field, which paves the way for the content of the subsequent chapters. Then, we introduce the concept of blockchain and its applications in the agricultural field, which paves the way for the content of the subsequent chapters. In Chapter 4, we introduce to the readers why the green data center produces "centralization", and why the blockchain produces "decentralization". Based on the dialectic perspective, we think that both extreme centralization and extreme decentralization are not needed, and it is better to have a moderate combination of the two. We demonstrate to readers that green data centers and blockchains are general purpose technologies (GPTs) with pervasiveness, and they can be effectively combined through Zhongyong guides. In Chapter 5, we first introduce the difference between the Zhongyong and eclecticism, egalitarianism, and compromise to the readers, and then distinguish the difference between the Zhongyong and similar or easily confused philosophical concepts. The integration between the green data center and the blockchain should be completed through the practicality of Zhongyong. Then, we introduce the three conditions for practicing the Zhongyong: multifaceted thinking, integration of decision-making, and harmony of implementation. Based on these three conditions, we analyze the practicality of integrating green data center and blockchain technology based on the Zhongyong. In

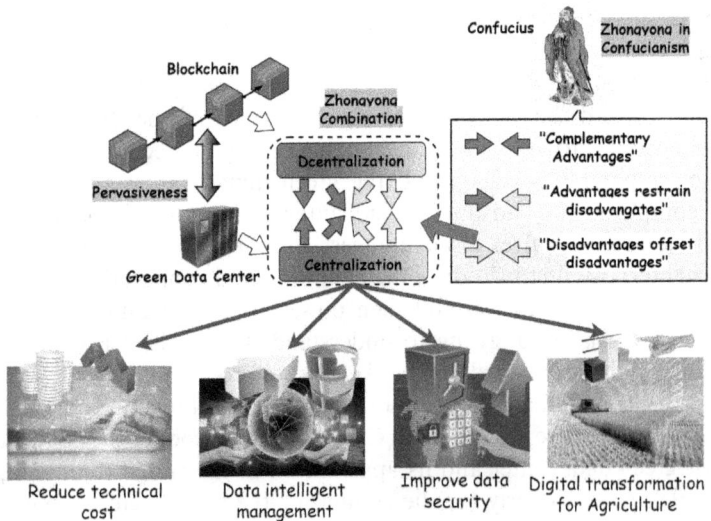

Figure 2.8 Schematic diagram of the research framework.

Chapter 6, we introduce the development status, brilliance, and current difficulties of Beijing Liuminying Ecological Farm as a case and provide an entry point for the case study. Based on this, we propose a digital circular agriculture framework based on the green data center and the blockchain. This framework contains sufficient Zhongyong. Finally, we use four of the six commonly used Zhongyong logics, combining the advantages of the green data center and the blockchain itself, and present a detailed analysis of the framework, as well as the overall potential benefits of the framework to circular agriculture digitalization. Finally, in the concluding section, we summarize the research content of the book, put forward the remaining shortcomings of the research, and provide new directions for looking into the future. We encourage philosophical and technical logic to try bolder "hugs" to provide innovative solutions and outstanding wisdom for further solving the problem of agricultural digitalization. The research framework is shown in Figure 2.8.

References

Blair, H.W., 1996. Democracy, equity and common property resource management in the Indian subcontinent. *Development and Change* 27(3), 475–499.

Chen, Y., Pereira, I., Patel, P.C., 2020b. Decentralized governance of digital platforms. *Journal of Management*, Article Number: 0149206320916755.

Du, K., Dai, Y., 2018. The doctrine of the mean: Reference groups and public information systems development. *Journal of Strategic Information Systems* 27(3), 257–273.

He, S.J., 2000. An important topic on the cultural comparison between China and Britain: Compromise and empiricism. *Journal of Shenzhen University (Human & Social Science)* 27(2), 56–63 (in Chinese).

Key Concepts in Chinese Thought and Culture, 2020. Key concepts—Termbases—Zhongyong (Golden mean). www.chinesethought.cn/EN/shuyu_show.aspx?shuyu_id=2179

Qin, Z., Wang, Y., 2011. Comparison between integrative thinking and the golden mean. Lecture Notes in Management Science, 2011 International Conference on Physical Education and Society Management (ICPESM 2011), Hong Kong, People's Republic of China, 2, 257–273.

Witesman, E.M., Wise, C.R., 2009. The centralization/decentralization paradox in civil service reform: How government structure affects democratic training of civil servants. *Public Administration Review* 69(1), 116–127.

Zhou, Z.J., Hu, L.X, Sun, C.C., et al., 2019. The effect of Zhongyong thinking on remote association thinking: An EEG study. *Frontiers in Psychology* 10, Article Number: 207.

Zhou, Z.J., Zhang, H.P., Li, M.Z., et al., 2020. The effects of Zhongyong thinking priming on creative problem-solving. *Journal of Creative Behavior*, DOI:10.1002/jocb.441

Zi, S., 2016. *The Doctrine of the Mean: The Great Learning.* Translated by Legge., J. Zhongzhou Ancient Books Publishing House, Henan, 4–13.

3 Green Data Center and Blockchain

A Systematic Overview

The data center includes general data center, modular data center, all-in-one data center, and integrated data center. As the carrier and transport entity of terminal massive data, it supports the development of cloud computing, big data, IoT, and other cutting-edge digital technologies. It is the cornerstone of the informational society and one of the comprehensive embodiments of the national informatization strength. The scale and computing capacity of the data center will be one of the important indicators of informational competitiveness between countries. In 2020, the number of data centers above designated size in China is expected to exceed 80,000, the total floor area is expected to exceed 30 million m², and the year-on-year growth rate of data center-related market shares will reach 30% (CNITSN et al., 2019).

However, traditional data centers consume energy increasingly (Jones, 2018). It is predicted that the world's data centers will consume 500 billion kilowatt-hours (kWH) in 2020 (Bashroush and Lawrence, 2020), which will be intensified with the rise of blockchain and cryptocurrency (De Vries, 2018). The annual power consumption of China's data centers will reach 267 billion kWH in 2023 (Greenpeace East Asia, 2019a). In terms of energy structure, up to 73% of the power consumption of China's data center comes from coal power (coal as raw material) and renewable energy power generation (renewable energy as raw material) accounts for 23%, less than one-third of coal power (Greenpeace East Asia, 2019b). The dominant coal power generation has brought damage to the environment (Tong et al., 2018; Liang et al., 2018; Chen et al., 2020a), which puts pressure on energy conservation and

DOI: 10.4324/9781003369660-3

emission reduction. Besides, many traditional data centers built in China have some defects, such as overplanning of power supply and refrigeration facility, disorderly spatial layout, low efficiency of airflow pattern, redundancy of central processing unit (CPU) availability, and complicated cable arrangement (Zhang and Wen, 2017), which further aggravates the energy consumption, human resource allocation, and capital investment in the daily operation of the data center. Therefore, to reduce pollution, conserve energy (mainly electric power), save cost, and improve work efficiency, the development of green data center has been proposed and supported by the Chinese government and all social circles.

At present, there is no unified definition of the green data center in China. but it can be summarized according to the existing evaluation standards of the green data center. Based on the guidelines or documents issued by Chinese governmental subdivisions and professional associations (Ministry of Industry and Information Technology of the People's Republic of China, 2015; Ministry of Housing and Urban–Rural Development of the People's Republic of China, 2015; The Central People's Government of the People's Republic of China, 2017) combined with the existing research in academic circles (Wang and Khan, 2013; Oro et al., 2016; Rong et al., 2016; P. Huang et al., 2020), the green data center can be defined as:

> a data center that minimizes the negative impact on the environment and maximizes the sustainable utilization of resources from the aspects of building planning, energy consumption, and emission, waste treatment, operation management, etc., on the premise of ensuring the security and reliability of services.

In China, green data center technology has developed more mature products, such as the *Fusion Module 500* smart minidata center developed by Huawei. These green data centers mostly adopt the integration mode, which integrates the network cabinet, refrigeration system, power supply, and distribution system, monitoring system, fire protection system, and conductor arrangement into a box or container, forming a data center with compact structure, scientific planning, and high space utilization. In addition to Huawei, ZTE, Dell, KELONG, Microsoft, Apple, and other brands have also developed or planned a variety of green data center products, enriching the market. Furthermore, the global academic community has also shown a high degree of enthusiasm for research on the green data center, including floor thermal management (Zhang et al., 2019), cooling load and energy-saving estimation (Ham et al., 2015), research on component performance and life (Moghaddam et al., 2017), comparison of cooling systems (Khalid et al., 2017), and detection and optimization of device parameters (Berezovskaya et al., 2020). There are still many related types of research, but most of them focus on the design and planning, function improvement, and system architecture of green data centers, and there are few application cases in agricultural scenarios. A forward-looking application comes from an enterprise: In 2019, Canadian Agriculture Thermal Energy Corporation announced that it would build a 49 megawatt (MW) super large-scale green data center in an agricultural heat station park in Beauharnois, Québec, Canada, including many innovative patented devices such as passive-cooling ground-coupled heat-exchanger and sealed negative pressure cabinets. The data center runs the organic planting greenhouse through the heat generated by the servers (Intrado GlobeNewswire, 2019).

Blockchain appeared later, but it has a more rapid development momentum. The concept of blockchain appeared in Bitcoin White Paper for the first time in 2008 (Nakamoto, 2008). Once it came out, it has attracted the attention of all sectors of the society. Many scholars believe that blockchain is a technology that can push forward human scientific development and has great prospects (Extance, 2017; Anonymous, 2018; Wong et al., 2019). Blockchain has been popular all over the world and will eventually become the mainstream application technology (Deloitte Insights, 2020). The development of information and communication technology (ICT) has impelled the conventional computer-aided industry into an intelligent industry with data-driven decision-making (Lade et al., 2017). Blockchain is a digital technology derived from this development process, which has the characteristics of decentralization, openness, self-organization, and sharing. However, there is no exact and unified definition of blockchain, and many scholars regard it as an abstract distributed ledger technology (Seow, 2020). From a purely technical point of view, blockchain can be considered as a combined architecture and integrated product of multiple technologies, or it can be understood as a cutting-edge digital technology includes storage carrier, which is composed of the distributed database with block form, taking peer-to-peer (P2P) network as the communication carrier, with cryptography as the secure carrier, and ensuring the consistency through the distributed systemic consensus framework, which aims to construct a value exchange system. It can be applied to all scenarios with historical or holistic data recording requirements.

The application research of blockchain in the agricultural field has also aroused strong academic interest. A series of extensive studies include the role of blockchain in the Agricultural IoT (Ferrag et al., 2020), the blockchain platform based on the secure storage of agricultural data (L. Huang et al., 2020), the traceability of food safety (Ahmed and Ten Broek, 2017), and the application of blockchain in the food supply chain (Kohler and Pizzol, 2020). China also attaches great importance to the development of blockchain. In 2019, the Chinese government issued many relevant policies benefiting application, supervision, and other aspects of blockchain technology (Intelligent Manufacturing Network, 2019). At the provincial level, local governments have also successively issued a series of special policies for blockchain in 2020, proposing many landing-application fields and scenarios, involving finance, manufacturing, people's livelihood, government affairs, and communication (*Economic Daily*, 2020). In the agricultural field, a batch of agricultural blockchain application projects has also been implemented in the way of "government-led and government-enterprise cooperation". Taking Liangli village of Dangshan county in Anhui province as an example, the village abounds with the famous pear "Dangshan pear". Abundant pear trees are planted in this village and tourists are attracted to pick them. In September 2020, this pear-rich village became the first "blockchain village" in China. The project is the first rural revitalization sample based on blockchain in China under the strategic agreement signed by Dangshan County People's Government of Anhui Province, Agricultural Bank of China Anhui Branch, and *ANTCHAIN* (a blockchain brand of ANT Group). *ANTCHAIN* provides traceability certification service, establishes a full link searchable sales network for Dangshan pear, and provides quality assurance for its brand. The circulation of goods, capital flow, and information transfer will occur synchronously in the chain, forming the credible data assets of operation entities, and providing reliable data basis for the precise service and supervision of the government (The Paper, 2020).

References

Ahmed, S., Ten Broek, N., 2017. Blockchain could boost food security. *Nature* 550(7674), 43–43.

Anonymous, 2018. Blockchain, meet genomics. *Science* 359(6377), 721–721.

Bashroush, R., Lawrence, A., 2020. Beyond PUE: Tackling IT's wasted terawatts. Uptime Institute Intelligence, Washington D.C., 2–8.

Berezovskaya, Y., Yang, C.W., Mousavi, A., et al., 2020. Modular model of a data centers as a tool for improving its energy efficiency. *IEEE Access* 8, 46559–46573.

Chen, X., Yang, T., Wang, Z.F., 2020a. Investigating the impacts of coal-fired power on ambient PM 2.5 by combination of chemical transport model and receptor model. *Science of the Total Environment* 727, Article Number: 138407.

China Electronics Standardization Institute, China National Information Technology Standardization Network (CNITSN), Sub Committee on information technology and sustainable development of CNITSN, Chinese Institute of Electronics, 2019. *The White Book of the Green Data Center* (2019). www.ictlce.com/wp-content/uploads/2019/05/%E7%BB%BF%E8%89%B2%E6%95%B0%E6%8D%AE%E4%B8%AD%E5%BF%83%E7%99%BD%E7%9A%AE%E4%B9%A6-210x297mm%E7%94%B5%E5%AD%90%E7%89%88.pdf (in Chinese).

De Vries, A., 2018. Bitcoin's growing energy problem. *Joule* 2(5), 801–805.

Deloitte Insights, 2020. Deloitte's 2020 global blockchain survey: From promise to reality. Deloitte, www2.deloitte.com/content/dam/insights/us/articles/6608_2020-global-blockchain-survey/DI_CIR%202020%20global%20blockchain%20survey.pdf

Economic Daily, 2020. Action plans have been issued in many places, and special policies for blockchain have been issued, www.ce.cn/xwzx/gnsz/gdxw/202007/13/t20200713_35304646.shtml (in Chinese).

Extance, A., 2017. Technology blockchain moves to science. *Nature* 552(7685), 301.

Ferrag, M.A., Shu, L., Yang, X., et al., 2020. Security and privacy for green IOT-based agriculture: Review, blockchain solutions, and challenges. *IEEE Access* 8, 32031–32053.

Greenpeace East Asia, 2019a. Electricity consumption from China's internet industry to increase by two thirds by 2023: Greenpeace.

Greenpeace East Asia, www.greenpeace.org/eastasia/press/1255/elec
tricity-consumption-from-chinas-internet-industry-to-increase-by-
two-thirds-by-2023-greenpeace-2/

Greenpeace East Asia, 2019b. Powering the cloud: How China's internet
industry can shift to renewable energy. Greenpeace East Asia, www.
connaissancedesenergies.org/sites/default/files/pdf-actualites/Power
ing%20the%20Cloud%20_%20English%20Briefing.pdf

Ham, S.W., Kim, M.H., Choi, B.N., et al., 2015. Energy-saving potential of various air-side economizers in a modular data center. *Applied
Energy* 138, 258–275.

Huang, L., Ulah, I., Kim, D.H., 2020. A secure fish farm platform based
on blockchain for agriculture data integrity. *Computers and Electronics
in Agriculture* 170, Article Number: 105251.

Huang, P., Copertaro, B., Zhang, X.X., et al., 2020. A review of data
centers as prosumers in district energy systems: Renewable energy integration and waste heat reuse for district heating. *Applied Energy* 258,
Article Number: 114109.

Intelligent Manufacturing Network, 2019. State-led, blockchain-related
policies in 2019! Intelligent Manufacturing Network, https://baijia
hao.baidu.com/s?id=1652432512833135574&wfr=spider&for=pc   (in
Chinese).

Intrado GlobeNewswire, 2019. UnitedCorp Announces Plans for 49-
Megawatt Greenhouse and Hyperscale Data Center Heat Station
Campus in Beauharnois, Québec. United American Crop, www.
globenewswire.com/news-release/2019/07/09/1880148/0/en/Uni
tedCorp-Announces-Plans-for-49-Megawatt-Greenhouse-and-
Hyperscale-Data-Center-Heat-Station-Campus-in-Beauharnois-
Qu%C3%A9bec.html

Jones, N., 2018. How to stop data centers from gobbling up the world's
electricity—The energy-efficiency drive at the information factories
that serve us Facebook, google and bitcoin. *Nature*, www.nature.com/
articles/d41586-018-06610-y

Khalid, R., Wemhoff, A.P., Joshi, Y., 2017. Energy and exergy analysis
of modular data centers. *IEEE Transactions on Components Packaging
and Manufacturing Technology* 7(9), 1440–1452.

Kohler, S., Pizzol, M., 2020. Technology assessment of blockchain-based
technologies in the food supply chain. *Journal of Cleaner Production*
269, Article Number: 122193.

Lade, P., Ghosh, R., Srinivasan, S., 2017. Manufacturing analytics and
industrial internet of things. *IEEE Intelligent Systems* 32(3), 74–79.

Liang, M., Liang, Y.C., Liang, H.D., et al., 2018. Polycyclic aromatic
hydrocarbons in soil of the backfilled region in the Wuda coal fire area,
Inner Mongolia, China. *Ecotoxicology and Environmental Safety* 165,
434–439.

Ministry of Housing and Urban–Rural Development of the People's Republic of China, 2015. Notice of the Ministry of Housing and Urban–Rural Development on printing and distributing technical rules for building evaluation of green data center. Ministry of Housing and Urban–Rural Development of the People's Republic of China, www.mohurd.gov.cn/wjfb/201512/t20151224_226089.html (in Chinese).

Ministry of Industry and Information Technology of the People's Republic of China, 2015. Notice of the Ministry of Industry and Information Technology, National Government Offices Administration, and the National Energy Administration on printing and distributing the pilot work program of the national green data center. Ministry of Industry and Information Technology of the People's Republic of China, www.miit.gov.cn/n1146285/n1146352/n3054355/n3057542/n3057544/c3634716/content.html (in Chinese).

Moghaddam, R.F., Asghari, V., Moghaddam, F.F. et al., 2017. A Monte-Carlo approach to lifespan failure performance analysis of the network fabric in modular data centers. *Journal of Network and Computer Applications* 87, 131–146.

Nakamoto, S., 2008. Bitcoin: A peer-to-peer electronic cash system. https://bitcoin.org/bitcoin.pdf, 2019-12-29.

Oro, E., Depoorter, V., Garcia, A., et al., 2016. Energy efficiency and renewable energy integration in data centers. Strategies and modelling review. *Renewable & Sustainable Energy Reviews* 42, 429–445.

Rong, H.G., Zhang, H.M., Xiao, S., et al., 2016. Optimizing energy consumption for data centers. *Renewable & Sustainable Energy Reviews* 58, 674–691.

Seow, K.T., 2020. Supervisor control of blockchain networks. *IEEE Transactions on Systems Man Cybernetics-Systems* 50 (1), 159–171.

The Central People's Government of the People's Republic of China, 2017. Notice of three departments on the evaluation of pilot units of the national green data center. The Central People's Government of the People's Republic of China, www.gov.cn/xinwen/2017-07/06/content_5208453.htm (in Chinese).

The Paper, 2020. The first in China! "Blockchain Village" landing in Suzhou, www.thepaper.cn/newsDetail_forward_9252166 (in Chinese).

Tong, D., Zhang, Q., Davis, S.J., et al., 2018. Targeted emission reductions from global super-polluting power plant units. *Nature Sustainability* 1(1), 59–68.

Wang, L.Z., Khan, S.U., 2013. Review of performance metrics for green data centers: A taxonomy study. *Journal of Supercomputing* 63(3), 639–656.

Wong, D.R., Bhattacharya, S., Butte, A.J., 2019. Prototype of running clinical trials in an untrustworthy environment using blockchain. *Nature Communications* 10, Article Number: 917.

Zhang, M., Wen, J.H., 2017. Research on the development of the green data center: Technology and practice. Science Press, Beijing, China, 11–12 (in Chinese).

Zhang, Y.W., Zhang, K., Liu, J.X., et al., 2019. Airflow uniformity optimization for modular data center based on the constructal T-shaped under floor air ducts. *Applied Thermal Engineering* 155, 489–500.

4 Technical Contradiction and Commonality

Centralization, Decentralization, and Pervasiveness

Indeed, through literature review, we can summarize a series of advantages of the green data center, such as stability, scalability, economic feasibility (Ham et al., 2015), design resiliency (Moghaddam et al., 2017), operational flexibility, and low energy consumption, which can reduce the adverse impact on the environment (Khalid et al., 2017). Despite the above advantages, the green data center is still unable to get rid of the inherent technical character of the conventional data center, that is, the centralization. As for centralization, we can try to interpret it from two aspects of technology and society: first, from the perspective of technology, a data center network (DCN) is composed of abundant host servers and switches. These servers and switches are connected through high-speed communication links, which will lead to resource centralization (Qi et al., 2014). The reason for centralization is that the software and components in communication network become complex increasingly, which will bring an incalculable load to the server and increase the comprehensive cost of information technology equipment (Schuff and St. Louis, 2001), the trend of centralization is obvious, and it is difficult to be easily changed in the short term because with the deepening of information technology equipment intellectualization and digitization, the complexity of software and components also increases (Rasch et al., 2019). On the other hand, from the social point of view, any technology should serve the public and avoid the technology gap among different groups as far as possible. In an organization, if information gatherers with special power accumulate massive information, they tend to be closer to the top of power than those information

DOI: 10.4324/9781003369660-4

providers (Gotlieb and Borodin, 1973) and have the ability to dominate information (Moller and Von Rimscha, 2017), so this is extremely unfair to those who are unable to obtain information because of technical or non-technical problems, especially those who advocate the grassroots technology movements and demand the devolution of power to civil society. Centralization gives some individuals greater power. Some individuals with the ability to control data will push for "centralization" further through the progress of ICT, and replace conflicting messages by penetrating messages, and finally through central control to heighten communication cohesiveness, and impose discipline on other individuals (Marland et al., 2017). Although centralization has advantages such as high leadership (Chen et al., 2020b), high efficiency (Zheng and Negenborn, 2017), and unified decision-making (Martin et al., 2016), it is often criticized and denounced. It is considered to be autocracy (or despotism), that is, the higher the degree of centralization, the higher the degree of autocracy (Chirumbolo and Areni, 2004; Pavett and Morris, 1995; Gibler and Sewell, 2006), and autocracy will lead to the defects of power rent-seeking (North and Weingast, 1989), information opacity (Miller, 2015), monopoly (Wright et al., 2015; Sadowski, 2018). After stepping into the digital age, when the centralization develops to an extreme degree, it will form a new trend. Combining the concepts "digital dictators" (Kendall-Taylor et al., 2020), "digital authoritarianism" (Tan, 2020), and "digital nationalism" (Callahan, 2020), we put forward the concept of "digital totalitarianism". It is defined as a small number of special individuals who can master massive data have absolute authority over non-special individuals in the digital society, and try their best to utilize data to control non-special individuals to establish a stable order. In addition to these few special individuals, most non-special individuals only have lesser private space and power.

In the digital age, digital totalitarianism will harm agriculture. A few special individuals (such as the oligopolistic enterprises holding supersized agricultural data centers) will store a large amount of agricultural data in their enterprises. Without strict legal constraints, these oligopolistic enterprises with supersized agricultural data centers will easily develop into representatives of digital totalitarianism. The actual controllers of these oligopolistic enterprises will influence the government's agricultural policy through data resources, intervene in the agricultural campaign program of political parties before the election, and even bring the whole agricultural industry chain of upstream and downstream into their control. This is like the landlords and squires in feudal China. They had a large amount of hereditary land in the country-side and could exploit the poor peasants endlessly. The agricultural essential productive factors of "land" became one of the sins in the Chinese agricultural history written by blood and tears under the feudal system. The landlord class who mastered the land would strongly resist any agricultural reform. The "Xining Reform" initiated by Wang Anshi, a famous political reformer in the Northern Song Dynasty, promulgated many laws and regulations that were helpful to the agricultural reform, but they were resisted and failed because they violated the interests of the landlord class in the whole country. If the productivity element "land" is replaced by "data", it is not difficult to imagine this tragic scene, that is, the oligopolistic enterprises that master the supersized agricultural data center no longer provide data services for farmers, then the farmers who realize digital transformation will not be able to use all the data information and digital-supporting technical services provided by the agricultural electronic trading platform, agricultural remote sensing satellite, and agricultural intelligent climate station. Digital agriculture will degenerate into traditional agriculture overnight. However, some gray data middlemen can become the rent-seeking brokers under digital totalitarianism, and they can act as a bridge between oligopolistic enterprises and ordinary farmers, to earn illegal profits for themselves. Members of the board of directors, senior managers, technical directors, and other employees with power in oligopolistic enterprises may also directly seek bribes from farmers to earn illegal income. Compared to normal transactions and services, we call this behavior "digital corruption", as shown in Figure 4.1.

This illegal behavior will greatly damage the legitimate interests and rights of farmers, and even use data as a chip to gradually turn farmers into digital serfs. Therefore, extreme centralization is unacceptable for agricultural digital transformation.

Although the blockchain has the advantages of openness, sharing, traceability, and self-organization, it will cause huge energy consumption, such as the power consumed in digital currency mining, which has become the consensus of most people in

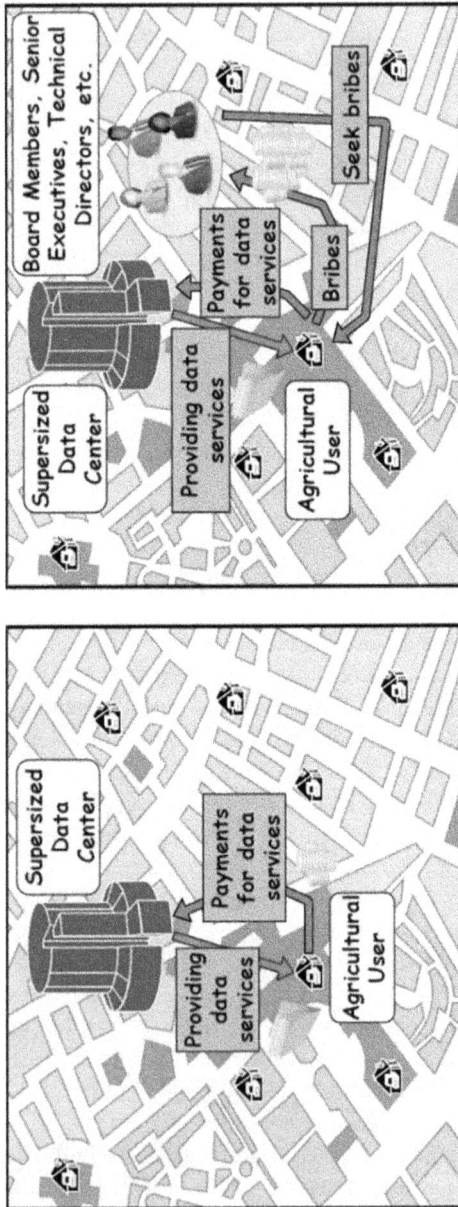

Figure 4.1 Comparison between normal transactions and digital corruptions.

the academic community or the industry (Sedlmeir et al., 2020). In addition, the inherent technical character of blockchain is decentralization, which is a contrastingly opposite concept to centralization. Decentralization has many advantages, such as more innovativeness than centralization (Kuhl, 2001), promoting competitive balance (Lago et al., 2019), reducing central control behavior (Eaton, 2004), improving the allocation efficiency of public goods (Olson, 1993), and democracy. Decentralization in the blockchain can also achieve decentralized validation to relieve the centralization pressure of institutions and reduce costs, without the supervision or intervention of a third party (Dai, 2019). The decentralized feature of blockchain can also prevent data damage caused by equipment failure and hacker attacks in the data storage center, which is conducive to information security. However, decentralization also has defects, such as low efficiency (Calabrese, 2012), fragmentation of collective decision-making power and executive force, and the decline of top-level cohesive force. Decentralization can be divided into three categories: horizontal decentralization, vertical decentralization, and physical dispersion-typed decentralization (Mintzberg, 1983).

Firstly, taking horizontal centralization as an example, it will give decision-making power on the command chain to other employees at the same organizational level, such as agricultural cooperatives or rural collective enterprises established outside the village committee. This mode endows some decision-making power originally vested with the village committee to the grassroots farmers, which can mobilize the initiative of farmers in production and give them more broad democratic rights. This has been more common in China and is beneficial to the development of agricultural democratization. However, the extreme decentralization evolved into the "people's commune" after 1958 in China. Excessive accumulation of public resources will lead to the fragmentation of collective decision-making power and executive force, and fall into the dilemma of absolute equalitarianism.

Secondly, if we take vertical decentralization as an example, it transfers the power on the command chain from top to bottom, thus gradually dispersing the upper-level power. This way can avoid autocracy, information opacity, power rent-seeking, and other problems to a certain extent, and can also increase the process of agricultural democratization, but it will also weaken the authority at the high level. The extreme vertical decentralization would inculcate a trend of localism, destroy the cohesion of the top, and distort the synergy between the top and the substrate. For example, the system of fiefdom was popular in the Zhou dynasty. The emperor expected to obtain the support of the feudal lords by devolving part of his rights and interests. However, the vassals who obtained the fiefdoms failed to carry out their obligations to the royal family, which eventually led to the fragmentation of the state and the destruction of the "nine squares" system (divide a large square into nine small ones, the eight outer ones being allocated to serfs who had to cultivate the central one for the serf owner), which represented the central agricultural policy of the Zhou dynasty. This kind of phenomenon has not appeared in China since the establishment of the centralized state in the Qin dynasty, but the local protectionism (this term is different from localism, which emphasizes more on the priority protection of local trade and will also hinder free competition at the regional level) scattered in rural areas has not been eradicated until now.

Finally, if we take physical dispersion-typed decentralization as an example, it splits the original organizational structure (including the command chain in the organization) and allocates the subordinate organizational units closer to customers. In China, the dualistic division between urban and rural areas was rigid and inflexible in the past. Especially in the planned economy, the policy of state monopoly for purchase and marketing abolished the original free agricultural product market, resulting in agricultural organizations only selling products to the government, and then the government sold them to the citizens. This made the government act as a commission agent and over-intervene in the market behavior. However, after the reform and opening-up in 1978, China's rural areas began to implement the system of contracted responsibility linking remuneration to output. The government returned the trading right of agricultural products to the grassroots rural areas. However, to decentralize an organization in a physical dispersion way, it must respect and accommodate any language, custom, law, or other requirements specific to geographies and cultures to provide tracking skill training and corresponding supporting facilities for employees of split organizations to support their future career development. Besides, when the structure of the original organization is disassembled and dispersed, and new organizations are formed one after the other, the growth and maturity of these new organizations need not only be cyclic, but also suffers from the continuous input of various resources, which is quite time-consuming and cost-consuming. The universality of Internet access removes geographical and time zone barriers (Staff, 2007), which makes physical dispersion-typed decentralization seem insignificant because the cost of popularizing the Internet and realizing informatization is far lower than that of physical dispersion-typed decentralization. Therefore, in the era of the high popularity of the Internet and information technology, extreme physical dispersion-typed decentralization can only "harass the people and waste money".

To sum up, extreme centralization and extreme decentralization are not desirable, while the right amount of centralization and decentralization is beneficial (Chen et al., 2020b). They can't be completely separated from each other and can form a certain degree of complementarity (Blair, 1996; Witesman and Wise, 2009; Mocetti et al., 2017; Agre, 2003). The agricultural digital transformation can promote agricultural innovation and enhance modernization of agriculture (Kelrkx and Begemann, 2020), while the realization of digital transformation often depends on the application of digital technology (Nambisan et al., 2017). The integration of digital technology into operation flow can improve the level of productivity and create novel modes (Trivelli et al., 2019). Besides, when the new technologies in a system are integrated, coordinated, or combined in a specific pattern, there is usually a significant increase in agricultural productivity (Kirkegaard, 2019), which is very beneficial to agriculture. Therefore, if the two cutting-edge technologies of green data center and blockchain can be adopted together, centralization and decentralization can coexist, their respective technical advantages can be taken into account and complement each other as much as possible, the technical advantages can be applied to restrain the technical disadvantages, and neutralize the respective technical disadvantages, then the Confucian Zhongyong combination between technologies can be formed and the role of "1 + 1 > 2" can be played. The premise is that both technologies have "pervasiveness", which means that there is a possibility of combining the two technologies. The attribute of general purpose technology (GPT) is pervasiveness (Bresnahan, 2010).

Therefore, if both the green data center and blockchain belong to GPT, there is a possibility of a combination between them.

GPT refers to those technological innovations that can promote economic growth, such as electric power, the steam engine, computer. In the engineering field, any technology can be a candidate for GPT (Helpman, 1998). Carlaw and Lipsey (2002) proposed three basic characteristics of GPT: first, it can complement the technology that defines it or supports it; second, it can complement the technology that can be realized through it; third, it can complement a group of political, social, or economic transformative technologies.

Compared with the above three characteristics, a green data center can be considered as a GPT. Firstly, the green data center meets the first characteristic. This is because the energy-saving requirements of the green data center make it bound to adopt energy conservation technologies in many software and hardware, such as information technology (IT) equipment, room air-conditioning system, power supply, and distribution system, and lighting system. These energy conservation technologies make the green data center "greener" and support the green data center. Conversely, green data centers can also complement energy conservation technologies. To save energy still further, taking IT equipment as an example, the green data center will adopt high-efficiency intelligent power supply, dynamic refrigeration, low-power CPU processor, and other technical components to reduce energy consumption, which has higher requirements for energy-saving of IT equipment under the requirements of overall energy saving and promotes the further development of IT equipment energy-saving; Secondly, the green data center meets the second characteristic. The modular data center is a kind of green data center. Its design architecture is based on the traditional data center virtualization application. It integrates servers, storage, and other devices into a compact structure layout. If there is no green data center concept, there will be no modular data center. The scalability and high energy utilization ratio of the modular data center complement the green data center, making it greener. Finally, the green data center meets the third characteristic. With the rise of cloud computing, big data, IoT, and the strong desire of human society for green development, the market demand for the green data center is growing. Big data and cloud computing are obliged to rely on the green data center to form complete technical supporting facilities. Big data and cloud computing can guide industrial change and industrial structure upgrading. They can initiate economic and social changes, so it's transformative. Green data centers can complement these technologies. Therefore, the green data center meets the above three characteristics and is worthy of GPT.

Compared with the above three characteristics, blockchain can be also considered as a GPT. Firstly, blockchain conforms to the first characteristic, because the blockchain itself is a technological product integrated by distributed ledger, smart contract, encryption technology, and other technologies. Taking encryption technology as an example, it supports the security of the blockchain. To further improve the security of data, the blockchain not only adopts conventional data encryption technologies such as hash calculation, digital signature, asymmetric encryption algorithm but also further adopts quantum communication technology in the future. For the blockchain, the more data, the more likely it is to become insecure (Fan et al., 2020). Without these data encryption technologies, the blockchain will lose its security and become secure no longer. Therefore, data encryption technology representing security can not only support the development of blockchain, but also form a complementary link with blockchain. Secondly, the blockchain conforms to the second characteristic, which is because the blockchain can realize flexible online transactions, and the surge in transaction volume also requires the blockchain to have higher technical specifications to perfect the transaction. For example, sharding technology is used to improve transaction processing efficiency through transaction sharding. Finally, blockchain conforms to the third characteristic, because it has been applied in many industry scenarios and has gradually changed the industry mode. Taking digital currency as an example, with the help of blockchain technology, it can bring revolutions to the traditional economy (Davidson et al., 2018), and an economic revolution (from traditional monetary economy to digital currency economy) can also be initiated by blockchain technology. Therefore, blockchain meets the above three characteristics and is a true GPT.

The key characteristic of GPT is pervasiveness (Korzinov and Savin, 2017). Specifically, pervasiveness refers to the potential of some specific technologies to be closely connected with other technologies, various social sectors, numerous production links, and assorted life-segments, thus bring about innovation (Bresnahan and Trajtenberg, 1995). Because green data center and blockchain are both GPTs, both have pervasiveness. With this, we have demonstrated the possibility of combining the two technologies, but we still need to explore and determine how to combine the two technologies and in what pattern, and whether the combination in this pattern is practical. Therefore, we fully learn from the Confucian thought of "Zhongyong", which can provide a more reasonable pattern for the combination of these two technologies compared with eclecticism, egalitarianism, and compromise. After introducing the "Zhongyong" thinking, we demonstrate the practicability of the combination through three necessary conditions for the Zhongyong practicability, and combine the philosophical logic with the technical logic, providing a complete theoretical basis for the combination of these two advanced technologies.

References

Agre, P.E., 2003. P2P and the promise of internet equality. *Communications of the ACM* 46(2), 39–42.

Blair, H.W., 1996. Democracy, equity and common property resource management in the Indian subcontinent. *Development and Change* 27(3), 475–499.

Bresnahan, T., 2010. General purpose technologies. *Handbook of the Economics of Innovation* 2, 761–791.

Bresnahan, T.F., Trajtenberg, M., 1995. General purpose technologies: "Engines of growth"? *Journal of Econometrics* 65, 83–108.

Calabrese, S.M., Epple, D.N., Romano, R.E., 2012. Inefficiencies from metropolitan political and fiscal decentralization: Failures of tiebout competition. *Review of Economic Studies* 79(3), 1081–1111.

Callahan, W.A., 2020. China's digital nationalism. *Perspectives on Politics* 18(1), 330–331.

Carlaw, K.I., Lipsey, R.G., 2002. Externalities, technological complementarities and sustained economic growth. *Research Policy* 31, 1305–1315.

Chen, Y., Pereira, I., Patel, P.C., 2020b. Decentralized governance of digital platforms. *Journal of Management*, Article Number: 0149206320916755.

Chirumbolo, A., Areni, A., 2004. Need for cognitive closure and politics: Voting, political attitudes and attributional style. *International Journal of Psychology* 39(4), 245–253.

Dai, N.H., Zheng, Z.B., Zhang, Y., 2019. Blockchain for internet of things: A survey. *IEEE Internet of Things Journal* 6(5), 8076–8094.

Davidson, S., De Filippi, P., Potts, J., 2018. Blockchains and the economic institutions of capitalism. *Journal of Institutional Economics* 14(4), 639–658.

Eaton, K., 2004. Risky business: Decentralization from above in Chile and Uruguay. *Comparative Politics* 37 (1), 1–22.

Fan, K., Pan, Q., Zhang, K., et al., 2020. A secure and verifiable data sharing scheme based on blockchain in vehicular social networks. *IEEE Transactions on Vehicular Technology* 69(6), 5826–5835.

Gibler, D.M., Sewell, J.A., 2006. External threat and democracy: The role of NATO revisited. *Journal of Peace Research* 43(4), 413–431.

Gotlieb, C., Borodin, A., 1973. *Social Issues in Computing*. Academic Press, London, 105–189.

Ham, S.W., Kim, M.H., Choi, B.N., et al., 2015. Energy saving potential of various air-side economizers in a modular data center. *Applied Energy* 138, 258–275.

Helpman, E., 1998. *General Purpose Technologies and Economic Growth*. MIT Press, Cambridge, MA, 167–192.

Kelrkx, L., Begemann, S., 2020. Supporting food systems transformation: The what, why, who, where and how of mission-oriented agricultural innovation systems. *Agricultural Systems* 184, Article Number: 102901.

Kendall-Taylor, A., Frantz, E., Wright, J., 2020. The digital dictators how technology strengthens autocracy. *Foreign Affairs* 99(2), 103–115.

Khalid, R., Wemhoff, A.P., Joshi, Y., 2017. Energy and exergy analysis of modular data centers. *IEEE Transactions on Components Packaging and Manufacturing Technology* 7(9), 1440–1452.

Kirkegaard, J.A., 2019. Incremental transformation: Success from farming system synergy. *Outlook of Agriculture* 48(2), 105–112.

Korzinov, V., Savin, I., 2017. General purpose technologies as an emergent property. *Technological Forecasting and Social Change* 129, 88–104.

Kuhl, S., 2001. Centralization by decentralization. Paradoxical effects in management teams. *KZfSS Kölner Zeitschrift für Soziologie und Sozialpsychologie* 53(3), 467–496.

Lago, I., Lago-Penas, C., Lago-Penas, S., 2019. Decentralization and football. *Social Science Quarterly* 100(1), 163–175.

Marland, A., Lewis, J.P., Flanagan, T., 2017. Governance in the age of digital media and branding. *Governance—An International Journal of Policy Administration and Institutions* 5(3), 37–48.

Martin, W.L., McKelvie, A., Lumpkin, G.T., 2016. Centralization and delegation practices in family versus non-family SMEs: A Rasch analysis. *Small Business Economics* 47(3) (special issue), 755–769.

Miller, M.K., 2015. Elections, information, and policy responsiveness in autocratic regimes. *Comparative Political Studies* 48(6), 691–727.

Mintzberg, H., 1983. *Structure in Fives: Designing Effective Organizations.* Prentice-Hall, Englewood Cliffs, NJ, 75–123.

Mocetti, S., Pagnini, M., Sette, E., 2017. Information technology and banking organization. *Journal of Financial Services Research* 51(3), 313–338.

Moghaddam, R.F., Asghari, V., Moghaddam, F.F. et al., 2017. A Monte-Carlo approach to lifespan failure performance analysis of the network fabric in modular data centers. *Journal of Network and Computer Applications* 87, 131–146.

Moller, J., Von Rimscha, M.B., 2017. (De) Centralization of the global informational ecosystem. *Media and Communication* 5 (3), 37–48.

Nambisan, S., Lyytinen, K., Majchrzak, A., et al., 2017. Digital innovation management: Reinventing innovation management research in a digital world. *MIS Quarterly* 41(1), 223–238.

North, D.C., Weingast, B.R., 1989. Constitutions and commitment—The evolution of institutions governing public choice in 17th-century England. *Journal of Economic History* 49 (4), 803–832.

Olson, M., 1993. Dictatorship, democracy, and development. *American Political Science Review* 87 (3), 567–576.

Pavett, C., Morris, T., 1995. Management styles within a multinational-corporation-A 5 country comparative study. *Human Relations* 48 (10), 1171–1191.

Qi, H., Shiraz, M., Liu, J.Y., et al., 2014. Data center network architecture in cloud computing: review, taxonomy, and open research issues. *Journal of Zhejiang University-Science C-Computers & Electronics* 15 (9), 776–793.

Rasch, R., Sprute, D., Portner, A., et al., 2019. Tidy up my room: Multi-agent cooperation for service tasks in smart environments. *Journal of Ambient Intelligence and Smart Environments* 11 (3), 261–275.

Sadowski, W., 2018. Protection of the rule of law in the European Union through investment treaty arbitration: Is judicial monopolism the right response to illiberal tendencies in Europe? *Common Market Law Review* 55(4), 1025–1060.

Schuff, D., St. Louis, R., 2001. Centralization vs. decentralization of application software. *Communications of the ACM* 44 (6), 88–94.

Sedlmeir, J., Buhl, H.U., Fridgen, G., et al., 2020. The energy consumption of blockchain technology: Beyond myth. *Business & Information Systems Engineering*, DOI:10.1007/s12599-020-00656-x

Staff, S., 2007. Centralization versus decentralization: A closer look at how to blend both. Chief Learning Officer: www.chieflearningofficer.com/2007/12/10/centralization-versus-decentralization-a-closer-look-at-how-to-blend-both/.

Tan, N., 2020. Digital learning and extending electoral authoritarianism in Singapore. *Democratization* 27 (6), 1073–1091.

Trivelli, L., Apicella, A., Chiarello, F., et al., 2019. From precision agriculture to industry 4.0 unveiling technological connections in the agrifood sector. *British Food Journal* 121 (8), 1730–1743.

Witesman, E.M., Wise, C.R., 2009. The centralization/decentralization paradox in civil service reform: How government structure affects democratic training of civil servants. *Public Administration Review* 69(1), 116–127.

Wright, J., Frantz, E., Geddes, B., 2015. Oil and autocratic regime survival. *British Journal of Political Science* 45(2), 287–306.

Zheng, S.Y., Negenborn, R.R., 2017. Centralization or decentralization: A comparative analysis of port regulation modes. *Transportation Research Part E-Logistics and Transportation Review* 69, 21–40.

5   Confucian "Zhongyong"

"Zhongyong" and Eclecticism

The Zhongyong is different from eclecticism. Eclecticism holds that everything that looks real, good, and eternal should be chosen to handle through an eclectic process (Kelley, 2001). In other words, eclecticism has two characteristics. First, it emphasizes that the objects in eclecticism are all positive and good, that is, only the positive and good objects can be dealt with in an eclectic way, and there is no dependency or opposition between these objects. Second, it does not emphasize the negative aspects of these objects. The above two points are completely different from Zhongyong. The Zhongyong can be diversified, but the objects are often antagonistic or mutually exclusive, which also determines that the objects in the state of the Zhongyong can have both positive and negative factors, that is, advantages and disadvantages of objects. For example, "wen" and "wu" in "neng wen neng wu" (*a Chinese idiom, Chinese phonetic transcription: néng wén néng wǔ*). "Wen" means literary talent, and "wu" means military talent. They have their advantages and disadvantages. They are opposite in Chinese culture, which is analogous to *yin–yang*. The Zhongyong is against eclecticism. In the *Yanghuo* chapter of the *Analects of Confucius*, the unprincipled peacemaker who insists on eclecticism is satirized as "the thief of virtue" (Wang, 2016). Another Confucian master Mencius also satirized them as "people who flatter everyone" (Yang, 2018). The Confucianists who uphold the Zhongyong believe that the eclecticism is wrong, because the Zhongyong not only emphasizes the impartial "Zhongzheng" (*a*

DOI: 10.4324/9781003369660-5

Chinese vocabulary, Chinese phonetic transcription: zhōng zhèng, "zheng" means integrity) and inclusive "Zhonghe" (*a Chinese vocabulary, Chinese phonetic transcription: zhōng hé*, "he" means harmony), but also emphasizes the "Zhongdao" (*a Chinese vocabulary, Chinese phonetic transcription: zhōng dào*) of fairness, justice, and science, and "dao" represents universal truth (Li, 2015). Therefore, the realization of the Zhongyong should not only have "Zhongzheng" and "Zhonghe", but also conform to the "Zhongdao". This is not a pure eclectic response of interests. The state of eclecticism does not necessarily conform to the standard of Zhongyong. The similarities and differences between the two are shown in Figure 5.1.

The first part (Part I) on the left side of Figure 5.1 shows the equilibrium under eclecticism, that is, at the midpoint of object-X and object-Y. This equilibrium is linear. In the process of solving the equilibrium, the two-sided or multifaceted characteristics of object-X and object-Y are not considered. The second part (Part II) on the right side of Figure 5.1 shows the equilibrium under Zhongyong. Suppose that object-X, object-Y, and object-Z are mutually exclusive, and each object has two sides. Red represents the superior side (advantages) and the green represents the inferior side (disadvantages). Take object-X and object-Y as an example. The advantages of object-X and object-Y can be complemented to each other, such as the careful thinking and prudent style of

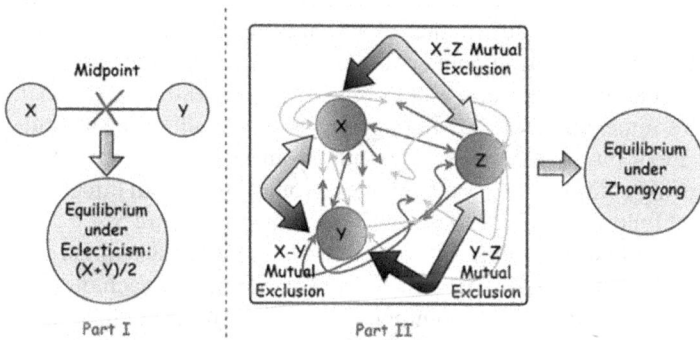

Figure 5.1 Comparison of equilibrium under eclecticism and equilibrium under Zhongyong.

"wen" and the courageous and resolute style of "wu", which together constitute the new advantage of "neng wen neng wu", that is, a cautious and decisive style. The disadvantages of object-X and object-Y can also offset and neutralize each other. For example, the cowardice (excessive circumspection) of "wen" and the recklessness (excessive bravery) of "wu" can offset and neutralize each other, and consequently, reduce the negative impact on the combination; The advantages of object-X can restrain the disadvantages of object-Y, such as the courage of "wu" and the cowardice of "wen". The advantages of object-Y can also restrain the disadvantages of object-X, such as the careful thinking of "wen" and the recklessness of "wu". In the same way, object-X and object-Z, object-Z, and object-Y can also be combined in this way. Finally, through this complex combination and interweaving, object-X, object-Y, and object-Z form the equilibrium under the Zhongyong, which is the outcome of mutual opposition and dependence of multi-level characteristics.

"Zhongyong" and Egalitarianism

The Zhongyong is different from egalitarianism, which is a kind of political philosophy, which holds that people should be treated equally in all aspects (Stanford Encyclopedia of Philosophy, 2013). Egalitarianism emphasizes more on a fundamental value-based on society and human rights, while Zhongyong emphasizes more on a criterion for regulating behavior or a way of thinking to deal with problems. There is no direct relationship between the state of Zhongyong and whether everyone is equal or not, nor does it involve the opposition and contradiction between different classes, different ethnic groups, and different religious cultures. The inclusive annexation of the Zhongyong is not egalitarianism, but a state of multiple symbioses, learning from each other's advantages, having complementary advantages, promoting mutual integration, and following the rule objectively, as shown in Figure 5.2.

The first part (Part I) on the left in Figure 5.2 shows the equilibrium under egalitarianism. There are four actors, each of whom puts forward his own opinions. Egalitarianism gives these actors equal rights based on different race, religion, and gender because their opinions are also needed to be treated equally. But such opinions are often independent and hard boundary, that is, they

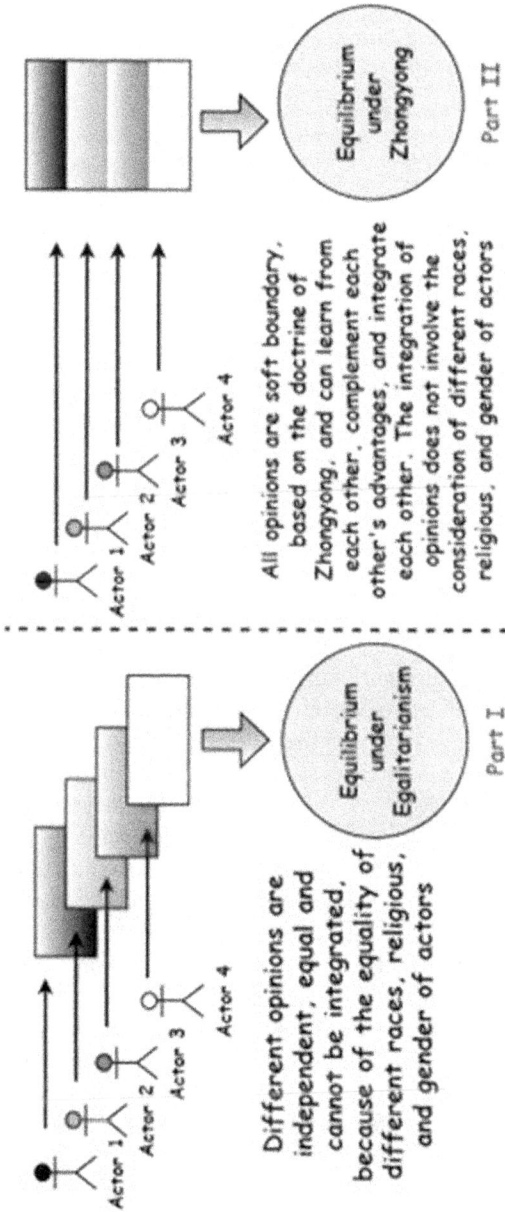

Figure 5.2 Comparison of equilibrium under egalitarianism and equilibrium under Zhongyong.

can only be stacked together and cannot be deep combined or integrated. The second part (Part II) on the right side of Figure 5.2 shows the equilibrium under the Zhongyong, that is, the opinions of the four actors are soft boundary and can be deep combined or integrated. Finally, their opinions are deeply integrated into a general opinion, and the combination or integration in the Zhongyong style is not restricted and interfered with by race, religion, gender, and other personal attributes or political symbols.

"Zhongyong" and Compromise

The Zhongyong is different from compromise. Compromise is more often used in politics, such as the term "political compromise". Compromise is often out of personal profit, but also out of respect for differences, and moral legitimacy is attributed to the moral commitment of opponents (Lister, 2007; May, 2005; Moody-Adams, 2018), with a sense of superiority formed by moral satisfaction. The transfer of profits in compromise does not take collective profits as the premise, but aims at personal profits and moral satisfaction, lacking common profits and value propositions. Equilibrium under compromise is short-sighted and unstable. Zhongyong stresses that "the whole world as one community". This not only represents fairness and justice but also represents the common value and collective basic consensus, which is also the greatest collective profit of the Zhongyong. To construct a long-term mechanism, all parties should actively maintain the common value and collective basic consensus. Confucianists realize that it is dangerous to compromise strategically for personal profits, and the harmonious order will not last long or even difficult to realize. On the contrary, it will endanger the "symbiosis" situation and the long-term survival of the stakeholders themselves. As a rational strategy and coordination method, harmonization for the sake of the public without favoritism, which does not harm the innocent, does not easily resort to violence, and respects every party with reasonable profit demands, which shows the unique public value of the Zhongyong, as shown in Figure 5.3.

Therefore, the Zhongyong is different from eclecticism, egalitarianism, and compromise, but a philosophy containing "harmonious proportional aesthetic feeling" (Yang, 2009). Compared with eclecticism, egalitarianism, and compromise, the

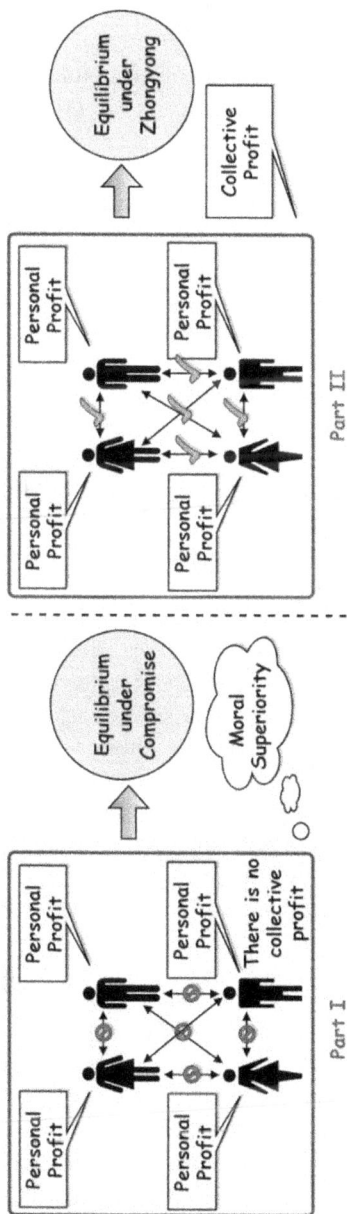

Figure 5.3 Comparison of equilibrium under compromise and equilibrium under Zhongyong.

combination of objects under the Zhongyong is more scientific and reasonable. Besides, "complementary advantages, advantages restrain disadvantages, and disadvantages offset disadvantages" is the unique feature and goal of combining objects under the Zhongyong, which has been introduced in the difference between the Zhongyong and eclecticism.

The conditions for the realization of the Zhongyong are complex, exceed the realization of compromise, equalitarianism, and compromise. Therefore, whether it is a green data center or blockchain, the combination of these two technologies to achieve the goal of "complementary advantages, advantages restrain disadvantages, and disadvantages offset disadvantages" conforms to Zhongyong thinking, that is, it is completely feasible in theory, but if we want to practice, we still need to meet the conditions of practice. When practiced in a world with volatility, uncertainty, complexity, and ambiguity, the difficulties or challenges it faces are self-evident (Di Giacomo et al., 2017; Millar et al., 2018; Schoemaker et al., 2018). Globalization has led to an explosion of massive data in every corner of society (Yuan and Tian, 2019). Therefore, systematic, flexible, and efficient cognitive processing ability has become an essential practical ability in the digital age (Ferras-Hernandez, 2018; Ryden and EI Sawy, 2019). It is of great significance to carry out practice with the thinking of Zhongyong. Compared with those who seldom use Zhongyong thinking, those who actively use Zhongyong thinking to carry out practice have a more comprehensive, flexible, and efficient cognitive processing capacity, and tend to use this capacity to actively interact with the external world (Chang and Yang, 2014). Therefore, using Zhongyong thinking to carry out practical activities is in line with the requirements of the digital age. In recent years, the Zhongyong is often used to study practical problems such as organizational behavior, business ethics, and enterprise management (Fiedler, 1981; Pierce and Aguinis, 2013; Provis, 2019) and has achieved success (Kim et al., 2004). However, these studies lack the prerequisite supporting conditions of generalization, universality, and unification, that is, they do not elaborate on the prerequisite support conditions for the practical application of the Zhongyong. Therefore, if the practice cannot meet the necessary conditions under Zhongyong thinking, then there is no logical self-consistency.

To apply and practice the philosophical thinking of Zhongyong, some scholars have refined and summarized three prerequisite necessary conditions for the application of the Zhongyong thinking in practice (Yang and Lin, 2012). First, before dealing with problems, we should have the "multifaceted thinking" of analyzing problems, that is, thinking from the perspective of opposition or mutual exclusion. Second, it's necessary to pay attention to both the advantages and disadvantages of different schemes in selecting implementation programs and form the selection strategy of "integration of decision-making". Third, in the implementation of specific programs, it's necessary to have the "harmony of implementation" to satisfy more audience groups.

First, although the green data center has the characteristics of low energy consumption, high efficiency, and high environmental protection, it will still lead to the trend of centralization, while blockchain technology has the characteristics of decentralization. Centralization and decentralization are two seemingly mutually exclusive technical features, representing two different technical aspects. Therefore, from the perspective of technology, before the technical framework constructing of Beijing Liuminying Ecological Farm, it's necessary to consider the centralization and decentralization concurrently, which is in line with "multifaceted thinking".

Second, the realization of the Zhongyong combination of green data center and blockchain can have the advantages of both, complement each other's advantages, suppress the disadvantages with the advantages, and offset their disadvantages to the maximum extent. For example, the autocracy and monopoly derived from the green data center under the extreme centralized conditions can neutralize the fragmentation of collective decision-making power and executive force derived from the blockchain under the extreme decentralized conditions. This is in line with "integration of decision-making".

Third, for agricultural practitioners, whether it is the supporters of centralization or decentralization, the conflict of views between the two groups is inevitable, and simply choosing any technical scheme cannot satisfy the other group. Digital technology must serve the public as much as possible to obtain sustainable development driving force and support. Therefore, the simultaneous and compatible use of green data centers and blockchain technologies can maximize the satisfaction of the two groups, which is in line with the "harmony of implementation".

In conclusion, the combined application of green data center and blockchain in agricultural digital transformation satisfies Zhongyong practicability (i.e., practicability under Zhongyong thinking). Therefore, in Chapter 6, we will propose a digital circular agricultural framework for Beijing Liuminying Ecological Farm, which can help it reduce technical costs, raise data security, and realize intelligent data management.

References

Chang, T.Y., Yang, C.T., 2014. Individual different in Zhong-yong tendency and processing capacity. *Frontiers in Psychology* 5, Article Number:1316, DOI:10.3389/fpsyg.2014.01316

Di Giacomo, D., Ranieri, J., Lacasa, P., 2017. Digital learning as enhanced learning processing? Cognitive evidence for new insight of smart learning. *Frontiers in Psychology* 8, Article Number:1329.

Ferras-Hernandez, X., 2018. The future of management in a world of electronic brains. *Journal of Management Inquiry* 27(2), 260–263.

Fiedler, F.E., 1981. Leadership effectiveness. *American Behavioral Scientist* 24(5), 619–632.

Kelley, D.R., 2001. Eclecticism and the history of ideas. *Journal of the History of Ideas* 62(4), 577–592.

Kim, C.W., McInerney, M., Sikula, A., 2004. A model of reasoned responses: Use of the golden mean and implications for management practice. *Journal of Business Ethics* 51(4), 387–395.

Li, X.C., 2015. The compromise spirit of "Zhongyong" and its political limitations. *Guizhou Social Sciences* 312(12), 23–29 (in Chinese).

Lister, A., 2007. Public reason and moral compromise. *Canadian Journal of Philosophy* 37(1), 1–34.

May, S.C., 2005. Principled compromise and the abortion controversy. *Philosophy and Public Affairs* 33(4), 317–348.

Millar, C.C.J.M., Groth, O., Mahon, J.F., 2018. Management innovation in a VUCA world: Challenges and recommendations. *California Management Review* 61(1), 5–14.

Moody-Adams, M.M., 2018. Democratic conflict and the political morality of compromise. In: Knight J (ed.) *Compromise: NOMOS LIX.* New York University Press, New York, 186–219.

Pierce, J.R., Aguinis, H., 2013. The too-much-of-a-good-thing effect in management. *Journal of Management* 39(2), 313–338.

Provis, C., 2019. Business ethics, Confucianism and different faces of ritual. *Journal of Business Ethics* 165(2) (special issue), 191–204.

Ryden, P., EI Sawy, O.A., 2019. How managers perceive real-time management: Thinking fast and flow. *California Management Review* 61(2), 155–177.

Schoemaker, P.J.H., Heaton, S., Teece, D., 2018. Innovation, dynamic capabilities, and leadership. *California Management Review* 61(1), 15–42.

Stanford Encyclopedia of Philosophy, 2013. Egalitarianism. https://plato.stanford.edu/entries/egalitarianism/

Wang, H.Y., 2016. *Translation and Annotation of the Analects of Confucius.* Confucius School Publishing House, Guizhou, 228–243 (in Chinese).

Yang, F.B., 2018. *Novel Annotation and Translation of Mencius.* Peking University Press, Beijing, 300–362 (in Chinese).

Yang, Z.F., 2009. A case of attempt to combine to Chinese traditional culture with the social science: The social psychological research of "Zhongyong". *Journal of Renmin University of China* 3, 53–60 (in Chinese).

Yang, Z.F., Lin, S.D, 2012. A construct validity study of C.F. Yang's Zhong Yong conceptualization. *Sociological Studies* 27 (4), 167–186+ 245 (in Chinese).

Yuan, J.W., Tian, Y.F., 2019. Practical privacy-preserving MapReduce based k-means clustering over large-scale dataset. *IEEE Transactions on Cloud Computing* 7(2), 568–579.

6   Digital Transformation Project of Beijing Liuminying Ecological Farm

As a country with thousands of years of agricultural civilization, China's agricultural activities began in the Neolithic Age (Ning et al., 2020). Even to this day, agriculture remains one of the main pillars of Chinese economy, and it shoulders the food needs of 1.4 billion people. Therefore, for China's national development, agriculture will continue to play an indispensable role, and food security is one of the red lines of China's national security. *China Newsweek* once published a long piece (Xu, 2020) on the impact of the global food crisis on China in the background of COVID-19. Although most experts are optimistic about China's smooth passage of the food crisis, some experts still put forward a cautious view, believing that short-term or cyclical fluctuations in the price of food supply and demand, coupled with the significant increase in the cost of grain production in China in the past decade. Some grain-producing areas are serious in degradation, and the sustainable growth of Chinese food is threatened. This news is not an alarmist talk. A joint report published by the United States Department of Agriculture (USDA) and Global Agricultural Information Network (GAIN) shows that the Chinese government recently adjusted its grain policy to meet growing feed and food demand, including reducing corn area, restoring double-cross rice planting, stabilizing the wheat area, and reducing fallow area (USDA and GAIN, 2020).

This global food crisis will force China to speed up the deepening of agricultural reform. In addition to adjusting agricultural farming policies and optimizing grain planting categories by administrative measures, it is particularly important to deepen

DOI: 10.4324/9781003369660-6

agricultural technology innovation and further strengthen the driving function of technology on agricultural innovation. Studies have shown that the emergence of novel products, novel technologies, and novel services can improve the production level and bring recovery to the industrial market (Archibugi, 2017; Hauser and Lindtner, 2017). China's development, research, and application of remote sensing, artificial intelligence (AI), Internet of Things (IoT), big data, cloud computing, virtual reality (VR), and other technologies have formed a systematic and mature system, and occupy the leading position in the world. Most of these cutting-edge technologies rely on data-driven, so they are collectively referred to as "digital technologies" (DTs), which provide support for the Chinese agricultural digital transformation. Among these technologies, green data centers and blockchain are relatively novel. Green data center is the technical carrier of the concept of "centralization". It has the advantages of stability, scalability, and design resiliency, while blockchain is the technical carrier of the concept "decentralization". It has the advantages of openness, sharing, and self-organization. Both these tools have been studied and applied in the Chinese agricultural field.

However, although the green data center solves the shortcomings of the traditional digital center, such as high energy consumption and high pollution, it is easy to lead to power rent-seeking, information opacity, monopoly, autocracy, and other disadvantages. These disadvantages principally stem from the inherent technical character "centralization"; similarly, blockchain is easy to lead to low efficiency, fragmentation of collective decision-making power and executive force, and decline of top-level cohesive force. These disadvantages mainly come from its inherent technical character "decentralization". Centralization and decentralization, the technical characters of these two technologies, seem to be opposite, but they can realize the Zhongyong (*a Chinese vocabulary, Chinese phonetic transcription: zhōng yōng*) combination to achieve the goal of "complementary advantages, advantages restrain disadvantages, disadvantages offset disadvantages".

Here we take Beijing Liuminying Ecological Farm as an example to explain in detail. The development and utilization of solar energy and bioenergy in Beijing Liuminying Ecological Farm have formed a one-stop circular agricultural system with biogas, planting, breeding, processing, production, supply, sales, and agricultural tourism (Daxing District Government of Beijing, 2018). This circular agricultural mode can use part of the renewable agricultural wastes as resources through the reasonable inner organization of the agricultural system, coupling the inner agricultural production links into a closed loop of material and energy recycling, achieving resource conservation and multiple utilization. It has the characteristics of improving resource utilization rate, eliminating external economic uncertainty, saving resources, and optimizing the agricultural production environment.

Beijing Liuminying Ecological Farm has won many honors for its widely praised circular agriculture mode and diversified business operations, including the honorary titles of "the most beautiful village in Beijing" and "national green village". However, with time, a series of shortcomings gradually emerged, including the media exposure in 2010 that its subordinate agricultural company used false product quality traceability codes, absence of pesticide residues test, and intentionally faked organic vegetables with ordinary vegetables (Xu and Li, 2010); In 2014, it was questioned by the media and experts that the production sanitary conditions of the organic vegetables were substandard, the organic compound fertilizer with over-standard *Escherichia coli*, and cultivation soils have antibiotic residues (Anonymous, 2014). In addition, there are also problems such as the excessive price of organic vegetables caused by middlemen's layer by layer distributed profit-making, bad smell of biogas affecting the organic vegetables' production environment and farmers' health, unsatisfactory water and soil quality, ill-formed production process, and unsustainable marketing mode (*Caijing Magazine*, 2014).

The crux of the above problems lies in the fact that although the Beijing Liuminying Ecological Farm adopts the green and sustainable circular agricultural mode, there is still a lack of openness, transparency, high efficiency, and accurate management in the aspects of production, agricultural cyclic process, and marketing. This not only leads to the tarnishing of its brand reputation but also makes its agricultural efficiency low, resulting in expensive input cost, lengthy payback time, and low output of organic agricultural products. Therefore, it is unable to realize profits to attract investors (*Caijing Magazine,* 2014). Therefore, it is necessary to improve the agricultural mode of Beijing Liuminying Ecological Farm to enhance its agricultural level. In October 2018, the Liuminying village committee proposed the goal of "modernization, scientization, and informatization of rural governance and industrial transformation", and called for close cooperation with the external world to build Liuminying village into a scientific novel village integrating low-carbon ecological style, digital wisdom, intelligent livability, culture-oriented travel, health care, and happy life (Think Tank of New Globalization, 2018). Based on the above background, we will propose a semi-centralized and semi-decentralized circular agricultural framework based on green data center and blockchain. This framework is in line with the unique feature of "complementary advantages, advantages restrain disadvantages, and disadvantages offset disadvantages" under Zhongyong thinking. It also provides a feasible digital transformation scheme for the circular agriculture of the ecological farm, which can improve the agricultural level.

The circular agricultural system of Liuminying ecological farm consists of several sections, including chicken farm, cow farm, pig farm, lotus root pond, fishpond, farmland, grain processing plant, biogas digester, and living areas. These sections will produce massive various business data in daily operations. These business data are usually collected and sent in the form of web application (app) or intelligent sensor. For example, the wearable intelligent health monitoring equipment used to monitor rinderpest and anthrax on cows (*SmartAHC* in Singapore, *Cowlar* in the United States, and *Agersens* in Australia all developed such intelligent sensor devices). This device can not only monitor the health status of cows, but also can use the global positioning system (GPS) to monitor the daily activities of cows in the cow farm. The cultivation monitoring equipment installed in farmland, such as the commonly used intelligent "farmland microclimate station", can be used to monitor temperature, humidity, sunlight intensity, wind power, and potential of hydrogen (pH) of farmland soil. The intelligent sensor installed in the vegetable greenhouse can measure the concentration of carbon dioxide and oxygen and provide accurate environmental controlling for the greenhouse planting of vegetables. When the business data is sent, it is usually received and stored by "my structured query language" (MySQL), "Oracle", "not only structured query language" (NoSQL), and other databases are deployed at the acquisition terminal. After data storage, the data will be imported into a centralized large database or distributed storage cluster, and simple data cleaning, preprocessing, and real-time stream computing can be carried out on the foundation of data importing. After importing the data, it's necessary to use the distributed computing cluster to analyze and summarize the data. Finally, according to the data after statistical analysis and classification, data mining is carried out based on various machine learning algorithms to obtain prediction, classification, clustering, and other calculation results. This process involves abundant calculations and complex algorithms, and the calculation results can provide more accurate data services for managers, producers, and consumers.

To better collect, process, and mine these data, we can set up mini green data centers in chicken farm, cow farm, and pig farm. The standard of the mini green data center can employ the design mode of all-in-one micro modular data center, which is composed of network cabinet, uninterruptible power supply (UPS), power distribution unit (PDU), monitoring, battery pack, and solar battery cabinet. Among them, a network cabinet can be used to deploy computing servers and storage servers. The standard of computing server is a blade server. Compared with tower server and rack server, it has the superiorities of low power consumption, small floor space, and low price of stand-alone server. UPS adopts rack structure and provides double-conversion online technology, which can provide customers with stable and reliable power supply, reduce the number of battery cycles, and prolong battery service life. PDU is a product designed to provide power distribution for the cabinet-mounted electric accessory. It has a variety of specifications, such as different functions, different installation methods, and different combinations of three-hole jack and double-hole jack. It can offer suitable power distribution solutions for different power supply environments, make the power distribution in the cabinet more orderly, reliable, safe, professional, and natty, and make the maintenance of power supply in the cabinet more convenient and dependable. The built-in monitoring is used to monitor the energy and operating environment of the green data center, which can provide 24-hour monitoring service. The battery pack is used to store UPS charge batteries. Solar battery cabinet is used to store solar batteries. In terms of refrigeration, the mini green data center has its cabinet fans and air vents, but no air conditioners were installed, that is, air conditioners are not

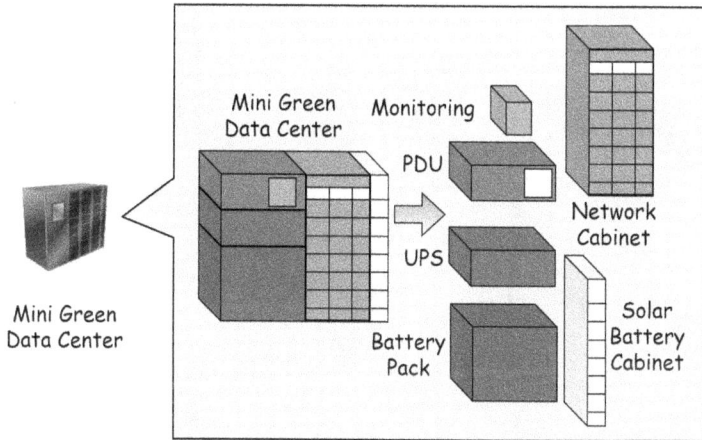

Figure 6.1 The structure of mini green data center.

installed in all-in-one micro modular data centers as modular components. Mini green data center adopts a natural cooling method, which can save energy consumption of air conditioning. The structure of mini green data center is shown in Figure 6.1.

Besides, different from the ordinary data center powered by coal, the mini green data center will adopt two ways of solar power supply and biogas power generation, to make full use of solar energy and biogas fermentation, thus it forms the sustainable utilization of agricultural resources. A complete "big cycle" scheme of green data center covers the whole ecological farm. Under the framework of "big cycle", cow dung, pig dung, sludges from lotus root pond, dry straws of farmland, and other agricultural wastes can be used as raw materials for biogas fermentation to generate electricity. The precise allocation of these materials can be done through the mini green data center, and biogas power generation can provide energy for the operation of the mini green data center. This scenario is shown in Figure 6.2.

All mini green data centers are managed by a management system. This system can provide highly reliable operation and maintenance and operation experience for data center infrastructure, and implement unified delicacy management for multiple data centers to ensure the reliability of data center

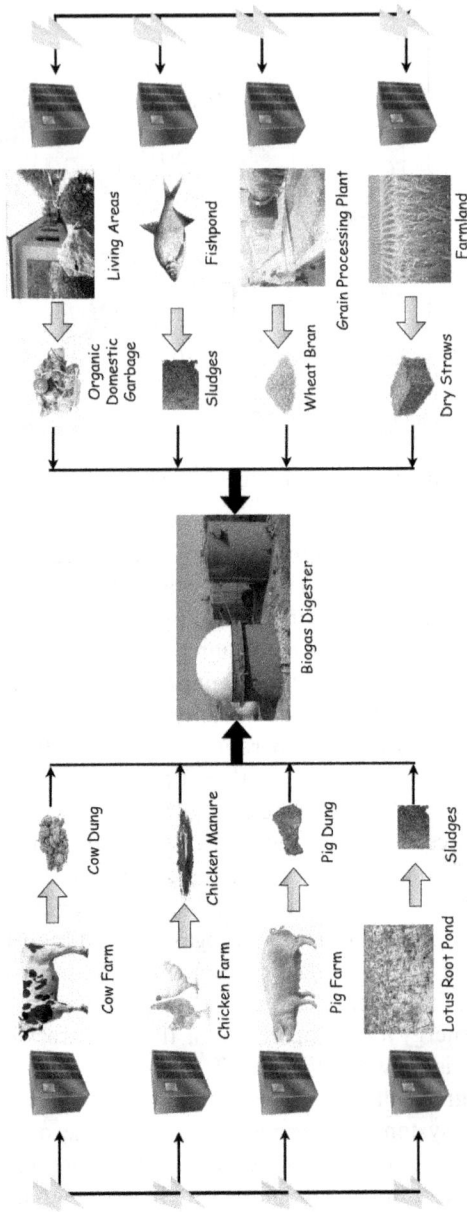

Figure 6.2 Collection mode of biogas raw material.

operation and maintenance process. It can improve the utilization rate of resources in the data center by using dynamic optimization methods for power, refrigeration, space, network ports.
Analyzing the operating conditions of data center tenants, it
also improves the operation and maintenance efficiency through
fault self-diagnosis of intelligent equipment, electronic inspection, and mobile app. This system can also utilize AI algorithms
(such as iCooling energy-saving algorithm) to real-time optimize the data center's energy efficiency. This scenario is shown
in Figure 6.3.

For each section of the cow farm, pig farm, chicken farm, lotus
root pond, and fishpond, an open "small cycle" architecture with
mini green data centers can also be built. Take the "small cycle"
architecture of pig farm as an example, we can understand the
application of agricultural digitalization in this scenario in more
detail. Solar panels are installed on the house (located in the living
area of Beijing Liuminying Ecological Farm) where the person in
charge of the pig farm. The solar batteries are charged through the
solar charge controller. The solar battery can be charged to UPS
through USB interface (path 1 in Figure 6.4), or from the solar
battery to UPS charge battery, and then the UPS charge battery
is used to supply power for UPS (path 2 in Figure 6.4). The UPS
charge battery is stored in the battery pack, while the solar battery
is stored in the solar battery cabinet. The whole solar system is
shown in Figure 6.4.

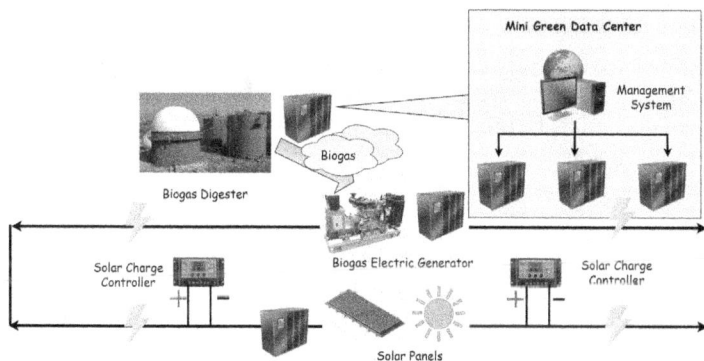

Figure 6.3 Management and energy supply of mini green data center.

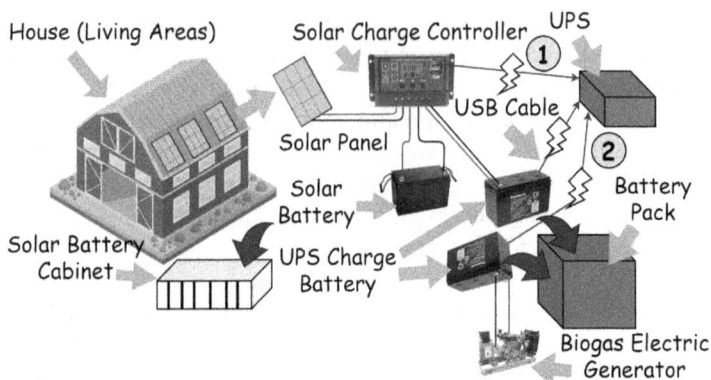

Figure 6.4 Solar system on the house.

In addition to solar power generation, human manure from toilets in houses and pig dung from hogpen are discharged into biogas digesters through sewers. Dry straw, wheat bran, organic wastes, sludges, and other wastes from lotus root pond, farmland (including grain and vegetable fields), fishpond, and other "small cycles" can also be poured into biogas digesters through inlets. Then these biogas materials are fermented to form a large amount of biogas and become the power generation raw materials of biogas electric generator. The electricity generated by the biogas electric generator can also charge UPS battery and provide power demand for the whole pig farm. The remaining biogas slurry and biogas residue in the biogas digester is discharged to the storage pool and transported to farmland, lotus root pond, chicken farm, and other "small cycles" by tank truck through the outlet, and then treated as fertilizer and feed. The whole process is illustrated in Figure 6.5.

Therefore, the circular agricultural system composed of one "big cycle" and several "small cycles" can not only strengthen the reuse of resources and the sustainable development of agriculture but also take data as leverage and new resources to form delicacy management and accurate circular agricultural mode through data calculation and storage services provided by multiple mini green data centers.

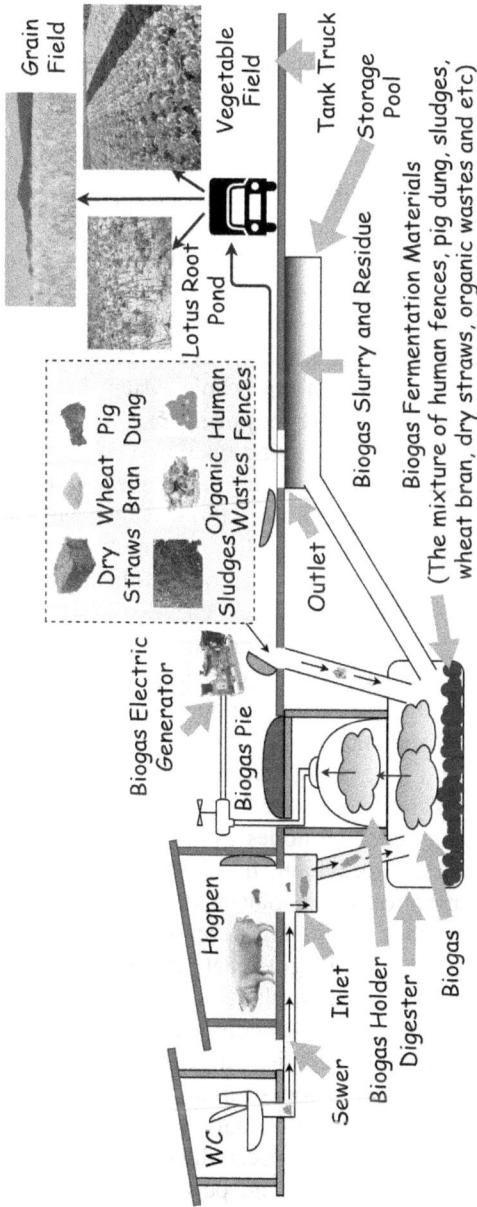

Figure 6.5 Based on the "small cycle" of pig farm.

However, agricultural digitization will inevitably lead to the exponential growth of massive data and lead to such problems as information island, data sharing management difficulties (Malakoff, 2004), increased risk of data security (Zscheischler et al., 2022). Whether it is a "big cycle" or a "small cycle", an abundance of heterogeneous data will be derived from each link of its agricultural cycle system in the operation process. There are some defects or risks in the storage, sharing, management, and security of these data, which directly or indirectly affect the digital upgrading and transformation of agricultural mode. Besides, even if the compact, integrated, and modular green data center technology is adopted, and the use of solar energy and biogas power generation reduces the consumption of petrochemical energy, the organizational structure of the whole system has become cumbersome and sophisticated, requiring one or more centralized equipment to support the digital operation of the whole system. On the other hand, a limited number of green data centers have the potential of "extreme centralization", which will lead to power rent-seeking, information opacity, monopoly, and even digital totalitarianism. Further introduction of blockchain technology can solve these problems.

According to the blockchain technology in Bitcoin and Ethereum, we regard the personnel in every section of Beijing Liuminying Ecological Farm as nodes, including pig farm, cow farm, chicken farm, fishpond, farmland, grain processing plant, living areas, and biogas digester. For example, tourists in living areas, shop assistants, and hotel service personnel, and farmers in pig farms can become nodes by downloading the node software dedicated to blockchain. In addition, if the wearable intelligent health monitoring equipment for animals, the microclimate station for farmland, the intelligent sensors for the greenhouse, the management system of the green data center, and other electronic devices applied to animals, plants, or agricultural facilities can be modified to be compatible with node software, these animals, plants, and agricultural facilities with electronic devices can also be regarded as nodes. These nodes can be broadcast nodes with only sending tasks or receiving information, miner nodes with mining function (need to download special digger program), or full nodes with all complete functions and permissions. In addition, each section of the deployed mini green data center will also be included in the blockchain system as a full node, and can be regarded as a "super node". Different from general full nodes, super nodes can directly contact the outside world and obtain information through the Internet, which will be described in detail later. No matter what type of nodes can be online or offline, all nodes follow the synchronous communication principle of blockchain. After the nodes are selected, we propose a blockchain structured system, which is composed of the data layer, network layer, consensus layer, incentive layer, contract layer, and application layer according to the seven layer-protocol-standard of open system interconnection (OSI) and existing research (Yuan and Wang, 2016). Among them, the application layer is the best to understand that it encapsulates various application scenarios and application cases of blockchain. In our proposed blockchain structured system, the application layer encapsulates the case information of Beijing Liuminying Ecological Farm. The basic technologies in blockchain are mainly distributed in other layers.

The data layer encapsulates data block, chain structure, hash function, timestamp, Merkle tree, asymmetric encryption technology, and digital signature. If the blockchain is regarded as a distributed ledger (DL), each distributed node can store a copy of the ledger. The data structure of this copy is composed of the data block, chain structure, and operation data. The authenticity and security of the copy are guaranteed by asymmetric encryption. Among them, operation data, also known as operation record, is the data generated by a series of behaviors in the Beijing Liuminying Ecological Farm, such as the usage times of biogas digester, the emission of biogas, the milk yield of cows, and the weight of pig dung. The data block is composed of the block header, block body, counter, and block size field. The block header encapsulates the block sized field, version information, parent block (prev-block) hash value, nonce, timestamp, difficulty, and Merkle root information. The block body contains all verified operation records from the genesis block. Each distributed node in the blockchain can encapsulate the operation data received in a certain period into a data block with timestamp through a specific hash algorithm and Merkle tree structure, and link to the longest main blockchain to form the latest block. The hash algorithm mainly includes MD (message digest) series algorithm, SHA (secure hash algorithm) series algorithm, and hybrid hash join algorithm. Merkle tree is a common data organization method in most blockchain systems. Its function is to quickly summarize and verify the existence and integrity of block data. This book uses the frequently used binary Merkle tree, which merges every two adjacent hash values of the first layer into a string, then calculates its hash value as the value of the non-leaf node in the second layer, and then continues to do the same operation layer by layer. Finally, the hash value of all operations is recursive to the root node of the Merkle tree, that is, the Merkle root, and stores the Merkel root in the block header. The timestamp is a key technology, which is used to record the write time of block data and provide digital notarization service for block data to prove the existence of data. It can ensure that all operations in the Liuminying ecological farm can be recorded and traced to the source to prevent the phenomenon of information opacity. The network is composed of chain structure between blocks, usually a linear linked list or directed acyclic graph (DAG). The advantage of DAG is that it can satisfy multithreading operations, but the disadvantage is that the verification time of operation is long and it is easy to cause a double-spending problem. Therefore, the linear linked list structure is still used here. The asymmetric encryption structure distinguishes the private key and the public key of the encryption system, so that the data sender X can encrypt the data by the public key provided by Y and send it to Y, while Y can decrypt the encrypted data through the private key, to ensure that the data is sent by X, while X cannot calculate the private key through the public key, which depends on one-way trapdoor function can ensure the security and unforgeability of blockchain data. The structure of the block as shown in Figure 6.6.

The network layer contains the P2P network, data propagation protocol, and data verification mechanism. Generally, P2P networks can be divided into three types (Liu and Özsu, 2009), namely centralized overlay, decentralized overlay, and hybrid overlay. In the centralized overlay P2P network, the central peer plays a role in promoting the interaction between other leaf-peers. Different from the C/S (client/server) network mode, although the authority between the central node and the leaf-node is not equal, all nodes can join or exit freely, but the degree of centralization is still high. There is no fixed network structure and no central node in the decentralized overlay P2P network. Each node is both

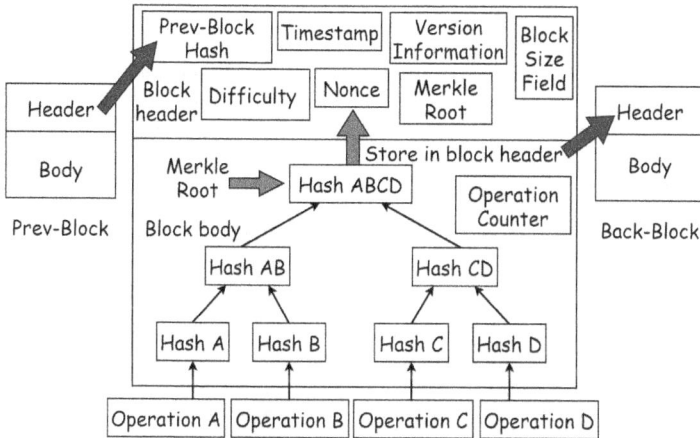

Figure 6.6 Structure of the block.

a client and a server. There is no uniform standard for the address of the node. Information can be exchanged directly between nodes, which is a completely decentralized network structure. The hybrid overlay P2P network is a hierarchical topology, and there are some centralized super peers. These nodes partially serve their leaf-nodes, and each super node is responsible for serving several leaf-nodes. The communication between the leaf-nodes needs to be carried out through the super node, which saves all the data index and storage location information. When the leaf-node X needs to download the required data, it needs to link to the super node for retrieval, and the super node returns the user information of the leaf-node Y with the relevant data, and then the data transmission can be carried out between the leaf-node X and the leaf-node Y. The hybrid overlay P2P network has the advantages of both centralized overlay P2P network and decentralized overlay P2P network. Compared with the centralized overlay P2P network, it has better scalability and reliability and compared with the decentralized overlay P2P network, it has a higher degree of support for complex queries. The structure of the three types of P2P networks is shown in Figure 6.7. As the existence of a data center will inevitably lead to centralization, we use a hybrid overlay P2P network, let the mini green data center play the role of the

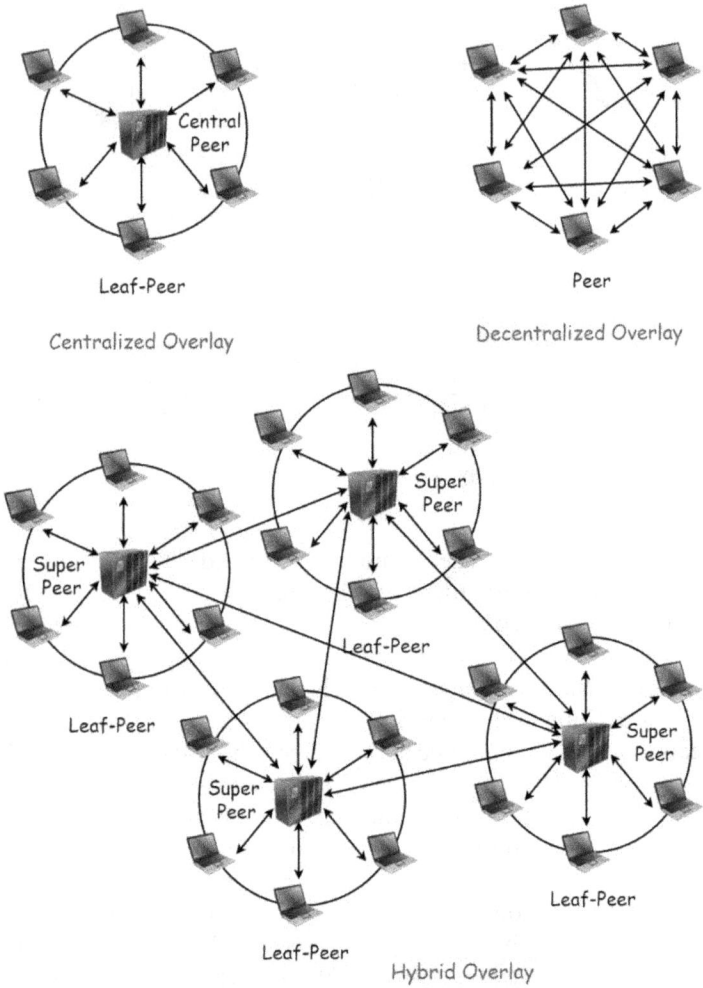

Figure 6.7 Comparison of three types of P2P networks.

super node, store the data index, and location of other intelligent devices and sensors. When data transmission is needed between nodes in the blockchain, the location information can be retrieved and obtained through a mini green data center, but these behaviors must be verified by all nodes to realize information transparency.

Data propagation protocol specifies the communication mode between nodes. The transmission control protocol (TCP) is used to conduct a series of operations, such as the initial connection between nodes, address broadcast and discovery, whole nodes synchronize block data and so on. When the new block propagates in the P2P network, each node receiving the block needs to independently verify it to prevent the propagation of malicious data or invalid data. In the P2P network of Beijing Liuminying Ecological Farm, after receiving the data from neighboring nodes, the miner node will collect and verify the broadcast but not confirmed data in the P2P network, and verify the data from the data structure, syntax normalization, digital signature, input, and output, and integrate the effective data into the current block.

The purpose of the consensus layer is to make the nodes in the blockchain reach consensus efficiently in the case of distributed computing. Although the more decentralized the decision-making power, the higher the degree of democratization, and the higher the stability and satisfaction of the system, but the lower the efficiency of reaching consensus. On the contrary, the more centralized the decision-making power, the lower the degree of democratization, the lower the system stability and satisfaction, but the higher the efficiency of reaching consensus. All kinds of consensus algorithms encapsulated in the consensus layer can make many nodes reach consensus efficiently in the case of decentralized decision-making, and all nodes have consistencies after reaching consensus. Different from the traditional distributed consensus algorithm, the blockchain consensus algorithm considers the Byzantine fault issue, which assumes that there are Byzantine nodes that maliciously tamper with and forge data. At present, common consensus algorithms in blockchain include practical Byzantine fault tolerance (PBFT), proof of work (PoW), proof of stake (PoS), proof of activity (PoA), proof of burn (PoB), delegated Byzantine fault tolerant (DBFT), and proof of luck (PoL) (Yuan and Wang, 2019). Among them, the PoW consensus algorithm is adopted in Bitcoin, which ensures the consistency of data and the security of consensus through the computing power competition of distributed nodes. Based on the computing power competition of their mining machines, the miner nodes jointly solve a complex but easy to verify the mathematical problem of SHA256 (one of SHA series algorithms). It calculates the hash value of the next block by the hash value and the nonce of the previous block. Whoever finds the nonce first can calculate the hash value of the next block first. The miner node that fastest solves this mathematical problem will automatically obtain the bookkeeping right of the next block and the Bitcoin award issued by the system. The PoW consensus algorithm essentially depends on the speed of solving mathematical problems by miner nodes. Another advantage of the PoW consensus algorithm is that its fault tolerance rate is 50%, that is, only dishonest Byzantine nodes control 51% or more of the computing power to launch an attack on the blockchain (such as a double-spending attack), which is very difficult to achieve in practice. Due to the mature application and development of the PoW consensus algorithm, and as the basic algorithm of many other consensus algorithms, we can adopt the PoW consensus algorithm in the blockchain of Beijing Liuminying private ecological farm.

The incentive layer includes the issuance mechanism and distribution mechanism, which is responsible for the issuance and distribution of token. Generally, there are many types of tokens, such as shares, currency, or commodities. We use the form of digital currency to name the token issued by the Beijing Liuminying Ecological Farm as the "green low-carbon coin" (GLCC). The distribution mechanism of GLCC can adopt the mode of the limited total amount, infinite total amount, or a mixture of both, and the distribution mechanism can adopt the distribution mechanism of enterprise operation system (EOS) or Filecoin (FIL), that is, the usufruct of resources must be obtained by the token mortgage. This kind of distribution mechanism can prevent GLCC from being maliciously hoarded and speed up the circulation of GLCC. Referring to the Bitcoin model and combining with the unique issuance and pricing method of GLCC, its ecosystem consists of issue, circulation, and market, as shown in Figure 6.8.

In the issue link, GLCC is open source, so it attracts many developers to contribute technology to improve its algorithm and mechanism. The miner node provides computing power to ensure the consensus and security of GLCC, and the computing power comes from the mining machine provided by equipment manufacturers. The energy supply of the mining machine comes from solar power generation and biogas power generation of Beijing Liuminying Ecological Farm. The blockchain network prepares a certain number of GLCC for each newly discovered

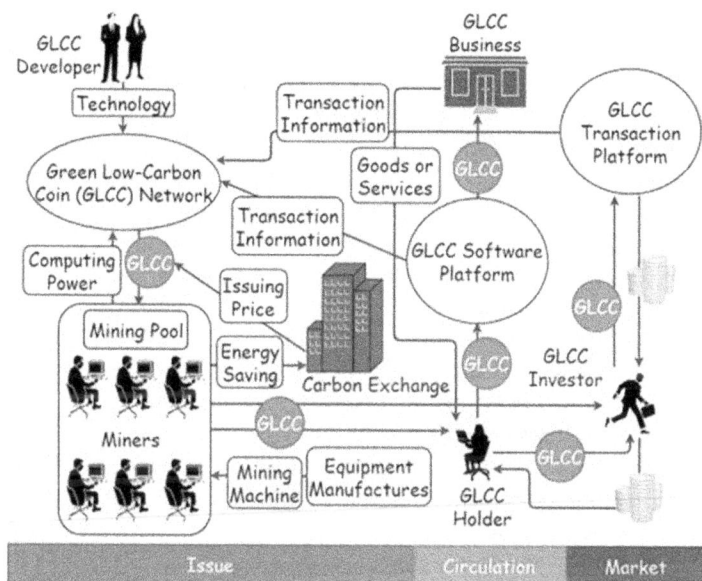

Figure 6.8 The ecosystem of green low-carbon coin.

block to reward miner nodes. Some miner nodes may cooperate to form a mining pool with revenue sharing and risk sharing to improve computing power, to gather scattered computing power, and improve the probability of digging out GLCC. The issue price of each GLCC partly depends on the energy saved by one token-digging operation. For example, energy-saving by using solar energy and biogas power generation to dig GLCC through mining machines (compared with the use of traditional fossil fuels). The saved energy is converted into carbon emissions through a certain formula, and then according to the real-time carbon sink price determined by the carbon exchange, the current holdings of GLCC, and other factors to make a price for GLCC. In the circulation link, the GLCC holders pay the merchants GLCC through a specific software platform (like Bitcoin wallet) in exchange for goods or services, such as organic vegetables produced by Beijing Liuminying ecological farms. In the market link, because the issuance price of GLCC partly depends on the real-time carbon sink price, it has volatility, which makes it have the attribute of financial derivatives so that the holders can sell the GLCC to investors, and the investors can trade through the GLCC transaction platform, and each transaction will be verified by all miner nodes and included in the blockchain.

Smart contracts are mainly encapsulated in the contract layer. It is a kind of computer program that runs on the DL. It can prefabricate rules and trigger them automatically, also has status and value, meets the condition response, can be encapsulated, can be verified, can be executed, and can effectively complete the value transfer and information exchange. As a set of procedural rules and logic of situation-coping, a smart contract is a decentralized, trusted, and shared program code deployed on the blockchain. The parties to the contract must agree on the contract content, breach conditions, liability for breach of contract, and verification of external data source, and can also detect whether the contract code is valid before triggering the contract. A smart contract can be independent of any central organization or third-party supervision. After meeting the trigger conditions, it will automatically trigger and execute the contract on behalf of each party. Moreover, the contract is programmable, and the participants can add any complex terms according to the agreement. The operation mechanism of the smart contract in Beijing Liuminying Ecological Farm is shown in Figure 6.9.

The construction and implementation of the smart contract are divided into the following steps: In the first step, the participant registers as the user of the blockchain, and the blockchain returns a pair of a public key and private key to the user. The public key is the user's account address on the blockchain, and the private key is the only key to operate the account. In the second step, the users write their promised rights and obligations into an electronic machine language. The participants sign the contract with their private keys, and a smart contract is generated, which usually includes the code, value, and status of the trigger condition. In the third step, the signed smart contract is transferred into the blockchain network and propagated in the whole blockchain network. In the fourth step, when the user initiates a transaction, the smart contract is called, and the contract code will verify the signature, and automatically judge whether the current scene meets the trigger conditions according to the verified and

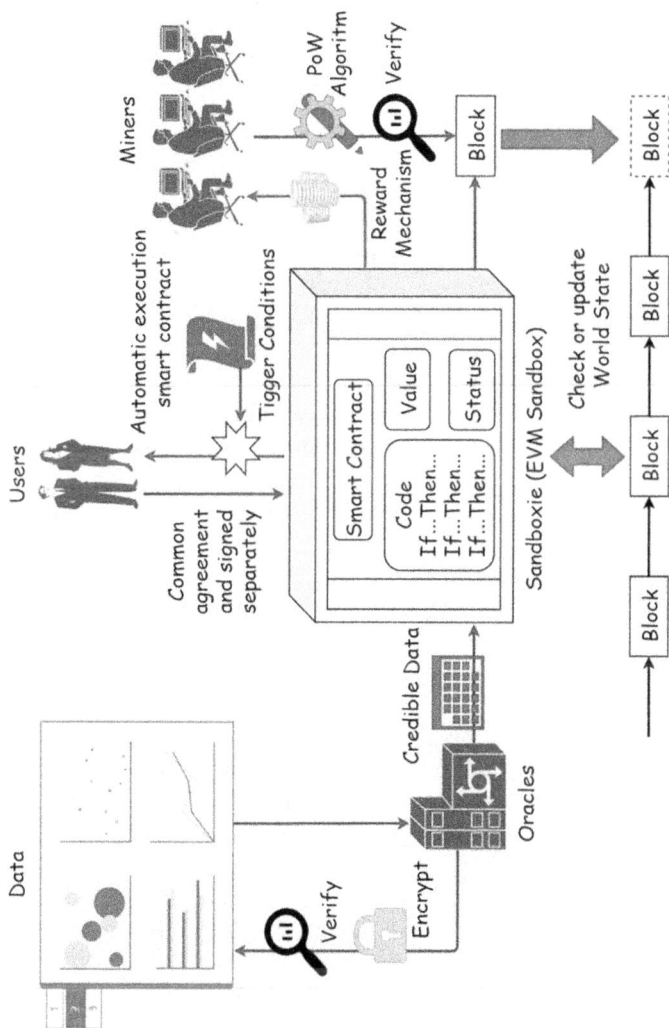

Figure 6.9 Operation mechanism of smart contract in Beijing Liuminying Ecological Farm.

encrypted credible data provided by Oracle and the information of world state checked, to strictly implement the response rules and update the world state. The execution of contract code is usually carried out by miner nodes in an embedded virtual machine (EVM) sandbox. In the fifth step, if the smart contract meets the trigger conditions, it will be automatically executed and the user will be informed. When all transactions included in the smart contract are executed in sequence, the contract status will be marked as completed and removed. In the sixth step, the completed executed transaction is packed into a new data block. Under the incentive mechanism preset in the smart contract, the miner nodes will use the PoW consensus algorithm to authenticate the new block, and the new block after authentication will be linked to the main blockchain to make the update of the world state effective. Through the introduction of the green data center and blockchain, we propose a semi-centralized and semi-decentralized circular agricultural framework.

In the previous section, we introduced the proposed circular agricultural framework based on the green data center and blockchain. It has two trends: centralization and decentralization. From the perspective of the Zhongyong, the advantages and disadvantages of centralization and decentralization can realize "complementary advantages, advantages restrain disadvantages and disadvantages offset disadvantages" under Zhongyong combination between the green data center and blockchain. For the "complementary advantages", there are "high leadership" complement "sharing", "scalability" complement "openness", etc. For the "advantages restrain disadvantages", there are "democracy" restrains "autocracy", "high efficiency" restrains "low efficiency", "openness" restrains "information island", "sharing" restrain "monopoly", etc. For the "disadvantages offset disadvantages", there are "autocracy" offsets "fragmentation of collective decision-making power and executive force", "digital totalitarianism" offsets "localism", etc. The whole framework and its merits are in line with the four out of six common philosophical logics of the Zhongyong (Pang, 2000a; Pang, 2000b; Fang, 2009; Wong, 1978; Pan, 2004; Tu, 1976).

In the first logic, "X is opposite to Y. Only X exists, Y exists, and vice versa". It means that Y can exist only if X exists. If X does not exist, Y will no longer exist. For example, "dong jing xiang dai" (*a*

Chinese idiom, Chinese phonetic transcription: *dòng jìng xiāng dài*).
"Dong" means motion, "jing" means standstill, "xiang dai" means
intercomparison and coexistence, "dong jing xiang dai" means that
motion and standstill are a group of relative concepts and whether
they are in the state of motion need to be set off by standstill.
Similarly, whether they are in a state of standstill needs to be set
off by motion. For the circular agricultural framework proposed
by us, the centralization of green data centers and the decentralization of blockchain are contradictory and interdependent concepts.
If there is no centralization trend, there will be no decentralization
trend and vice versa.

In the second logic, "Neither X nor Y". According to the concept of Cantor set, this is the complementary set of "X or Y",
which means neither X nor Y, but a simultaneous negation of two
states. For example, "bu bei bu kang" (*a Chinese idiom, Chinese
phonetic transcription: bù bēi bú kàng*). "Bei" means improperly
belittling oneself, and it is extreme self-abased. "Kang" means
arrogant and overweening, and it is extreme conceit. "Bu bei bu
kang" means neither belittling oneself nor arrogant, that is, neither
extreme self-abased nor extreme conceit. For the framework of
circular agriculture proposed by us, because it utilizes two digital
technologies—green data center, and blockchain—therefore, in
the whole framework, there is neither extreme centralization nor
extreme decentralization.

In the third logic, "Both X and Y". X and Y have no priority,
but they are parallel and equal and both exist at the same time.
For example, "de cai jian bei" (*a Chinese idiom, Chinese phonetic transcription: dé cái jiān bèi*). "De" means morality and "cai"
means talent. "De cai jian bei" means that one has both morality and talent. Morality and talent are equally important and
possessed at the same time. Morality and talent are all human
advantages, and they can complement each other. For the circular
agricultural framework proposed by us, it has two digital technologies: green data center and blockchain, and two inherent technical characteristics of centralization and decentralization, that
is, it has all the advantages and disadvantages of centralization
and decentralization. For example, the blockchain cannot directly
interact with the Internet world outside the blockchain, and its
scalability will be limited. As a super node, the green data center
can directly link to the Internet. When the blockchain is faced

with 51% attacks, in addition to using the asymmetric encryption technology and consensus algorithm of the blockchain as the security barrier, the green data center can also provide safeguards. In extreme cases, even if the total amount of computing power mastered by Byzantine nodes exceeds 51%, any green data center in honest nodes can send out early warning and require external intervention directly through the Internet in case of emergency without the verification of consensus algorithm. After the early warning is sent out, the propagation protocol of blockchain can be used to broadcast in the P2P network, so that the remaining honest nodes can know the intervention behavior in real-time. "High leadership" of centralization and "sharing" of decentralization form complementary advantages. The "design resiliency" and "scalability" of green data center make it accept refits of blockchain, which can be used for device login authentication, communication data encryption, operational order encryption, and so on. Based on the advantages of "sharing", "openness", and "self-organization", asymmetric encryption algorithms used in blockchain can distribute data among multiple servers. Besides, each block usually contains only the encryption hash function of the previous block, so it is difficult to steal the whole data by hackers. These are the complementary advantages of "design resiliency", "scalability" of green data center and "sharing", "openness", and "self-organization" of blockchain. Blockchain can realize intelligent management of the green data center, which can help the green data center maintain data security and data synchronization at the same time. Data center infrastructure management (DCIM) or data center management as a service (DMaaS) can rely on the DL technology of blockchain to assist more sites of green data center and tenants of server co-location, to implement more intelligent capacity management. If the green data center is incorporated into the blockchain as a node, it can save a copy of the DL. This decentralized storage mode can improve the security of communication between nodes and provide a highly secure transmission protocol for the green data center, which makes the green data center further improve the data security, based on the original embedded protection program. This also realizes the complementary advantages. Besides, the traceability of blockchain technology can record all records and status of the green data center, and blockchain can also obtain external data through the green data center to reduce the workload of Oracle and improve the efficiency of the smart contract.

In the fourth logic, "X, yet not extreme X, Y was taken into account also". It means that although objects present the state of X, it does not go to the extreme but also has the property of Y (Y is usually the concept opposite to X itself or its characteristics), that is, by incorporating some properties of Y to restrain or offset the negative effects brought by X and prevent X from going to the extreme state. For example, "yi rou ke gang" (*a Chinese idiom, Chinese phonetic transcription: yǐ róu kè gāng*). "Rou" means flexibility and "gang" means rigidity. "Yi rou ke gang" means to use the flexibility to strain the rigidity, to promote innovation and change, to prevent objects from becoming rigid. This is to use the advantages of flexibility to restrain the disadvantages of rigidity. Or, another example, "yi du gong du" (*a Chinese idiom, Chinese phonetic transcription: yǐ dú gōng dú*). "Du" means some detestable measures, which can also be extended to negative things. "Yi du gong du" means to use negative things to offset other negative things. In this way, both kinds of negative things can be eliminated, that is, disadvantages offset disadvantages. For the circular agricultural framework proposed by us, the advantages of centralization can restrain the disadvantages of decentralization, and the advantages of decentralization can also restrain the disadvantages of decentralization. Besides, the disadvantages of centralization and decentralization can be offset. For the "advantages restrain disadvantages", the use of blockchain can track and link the IT assets, power supply system, refrigerating system, space resources, and work orders of the green data center, and supervise the equipment and circuits of the green data center. The introduction of blockchain technology can break the closed data island, and then manage all system data, realize precise management of energy consumption of green data center, and build reliable energy-saving data monitoring and acquisition network covering all green data centers, so that energy consumption monitoring can be automatically collected and processed in periods, in stages, in production links, and in the supply chain. This is to take advantage of the decentralized advantages of the "openness" and "sharing" of the blockchain to restrain the "information opacity" disadvantage of the extreme centralization trend of the green data center. In addition, the decentralized advantage of "democracy" can be used to restrain the centralized disadvantage of "autocracy". For example, the consistency of the consensus algorithm of the blockchain can reduce the operation errors of a few managers in the green data centers' operation and maintenance. For another example, the green data center with cloud deployment can also use blockchain to improve operational efficiency. Although cloud computing itself is distributed and fault-tolerant, it still uses a centralized method to run, which has a certain degree of authoritarian structure. Due to the establishment of multi-nodes distributed database in the whole cloud network, the "self-organization" of blockchain will provide more independent operation for the green data center, and train the massive data collected by the green data center through complex algorithms, to extract rules from the diverse heterogeneous data and realize the intelligent self-organization management of the green data center. It can also reduce human intervention, improve operation efficiency, and enhance the transparency of the data center. The "openness" can also restrain "information island". Any full node in the blockchain can freely upload and download relevant data and can freely decide to join or exit. This open operation mechanism can make the data distribution more uniform in the P2P network and prevent "information island". For "disadvantage offsets disadvantage", the "localism" of blockchain under extreme decentralization can offset the "digital totalitarianism" of green data center under extreme decentralization condition to prevent data concentration in a few data centers and form monopoly. However, the "autocracy" of green data center under the extreme centralization can offset the "fragmentation of collective decision-making power and executive force" of the blockchain under the extreme decentralization conditions, to ensure the consistency of objectives, that is, to realize the digital transformation of the private ecological farm.

In addition to the above benefits in line with the Confucian Zhongyong, the use of green data centers and blockchain digital technology can also effectively solve many problems of Beijing Liuminying Ecological Farm. For the problem of using ordinary vegetables as organic vegetables mentioned in reference (Xu and Li, 2010), the green data center can shoot and collect all process data of organic vegetable production through monitoring and automatically upload these data to the blockchain for storage. The traceability of the blockchain can be fully traceable from the aspects of planting, cultivation, picking, processing, sales, and other links of organic vegetables, to improve the transparency of products for all authorized nodes (blockchain users) to query or download. It can prevent ordinary vegetables from passing off as organic vegetables. For the problems mentioned in Anonymous (2014) and *Caijing Magazine* (2014), the production management flow can be standardized through the smart contract of blockchain, for example, the specific matters and requirements of organic vegetable authentication standard are written into the smart contract and broadcast in the whole blockchain network. In case of breach of the contract such as exceeding the standard of *Escherichia coli* and pesticide residue, the punitive measures will be automatically triggered to punish the dishonest or derelict personnel. At the same time, the trigger of the smart contract can inform all nodes (merchants, customers, institutions, and others) on the blockchain network and automatically stop the unqualified agricultural products from flowing into the market, to avoid bringing more health hazards to customers. On the other hand, biogas can also provide power for the circular agricultural framework composed of green data center and blockchain through electricity power generation, so that it can continue to operate and form a new agricultural cycle. The transparent and open process management relying on the blockchain can also reduce the waste and pollution in the biogas fermentation process, and further improve the environmental quality of the Beijing Liuminying Ecological Farm. Besides, the high-density computing power of the mini green data center set in the framework is much higher than that of an ordinary personal computer (PC). As a super node, a mini green data center can play a more efficient role in the mining pool, greatly improve the probability of mining GLCC, and encourage more users to participate in GLCC digging. With the increase of the number of users, the number of miner nodes is also increasing, and the difficulty of digging coin (i.e., digging GLCC) increases. At this time, the general PC cannot provide the computing power needed to dig GLCC, then equipment manufacturers can sell mining machines to users. Although the mining machine has a high-power consumption, it can also use the solar energy generation and biogas power generation of the Beijing Liuminying Ecological Farm. Due to the utilization of biogas and solar energy, GLCC digging can further drive the blockchain users to carry out energy conservation, emission reduction, and ecological protection in the operations of the farm, tourism, and other links, and accelerate the development of circular agriculture in the direction of "greener".

References

Anonymous, 2014. The lies of organic food. *Consumption Quality Daily*, http://market.scol.com.cn/new/html/xfzlb/20140718/xfzlb702232.html (in Chinese).

Archibugi, D., 2017. Blade runner economics: Will innovation lead the economic recovery? *Research Policy* 46 (3), 535–543.

Caijing Magazine, 2014. Why organic vegetables are three to five times more expensive in China: Low price of ordinary vegetables. *SINA Finance and Economics*, http://finance.sina.com.cn/consume/20140714/114819695880.shtml (in Chinese)

Daxing District Government of Beijing, 2018. Liuminying ecological farm. www.bjdx.gov.cn/bjsdxqrmzf/zjdx/yzdx11/602656/index.html (in Chinese).

Fang, X., 2009. A comparative study of two doctrines of the mean between Aristotle and Confucius. Master Thesis, The University of Edinburgh, Edinburgh, Scotland, UK, 8–25.

Hauser, M., Lindtner, M., 2017. Organic agriculture in post-war Uganda: emergence of pioneer-led niches between 1986 and 1993. *Renewable Agriculture and Food Systems* 32(2), 169–178.

Liu, L., Özsu, M.T., 2009. *Encyclopedia of Database System*. Springer, Berlin, 91–93.

Malakoff, D., 2004. Data security. Report upholds public access to genetic codes. *Science* 305(5691), 1692–1692.

Ning, C., Li, T.J., Wang, K., et al., 2020. Ancient genomes from northern China suggest links between subsistence changes and human migration. *Nature Communications* 11(1), Article Number: 2700.

Pan, J.T., 2004. Liu Tsung-chou (1578–1645) and his reconstruction of Ming Neo-Confucianism. Ph.D. Thesis, The University of Edinburgh, Edinburgh, Scotland, UK, 27–95.

Pang, P., 2000a. Zhongyong and trichotomy. *Journal of Literature, History and Philosophy* 259(4), 21–27 (in Chinese).

Pang, P., 2000b. *Research on Confucian Dialectics*. Zhong Hua Book Company, Beijing, 79–100 (in Chinese).

Sood, P., 2018. Data sharing and analysis. *Science* 359(6371), 27–27.

Think Tank of New Globalization, 2018. Summary of the joint meeting of Zhongguancun and Liuminying rural organizations to revitalize party building. *Sohu News*, www.sohu.com/a/272029538_532369 (in Chinese).

Tu, W.M., 1976. Centrality and commonality: An essay on Chung-yung. The University Press of Hawaii, Honolulu, 42–117.

United States Department of Agriculture (USDA), Global Agricultural Information Network (GAIN), 2020. *Grain and Food Annual*. USDA, GAIN, https://apps.fas.usda.gov/newgainapi/api/Report/DownloadR eportByFileName?fileName=Grain%20and%20Feed%20Annual_Be ijing_China%20-%20Peoples%20Republic%20of_04-01-2020, Report Number: CH2020-0048.

Wong, P.Y., 1978. Philosophy of Hsun-Tze. Ph.D. Thesis, The University of Edinburgh, Edinburgh, Scotland, UK, 171–215.

Xu, D.W., 2020. The world is on the brink of the worst food crisis in recently 50 years. What is China's "grain policy". *China Newsweek*, https://dy.163.com/article/FMV2AGDT0514BE2Q.html (in Chinese).

Xu, Z.G., Li, S.F., 2010. Investigation on the organic vegetable base in the suburb of Beijing: "organic food" contains pesticides. *Tencent News*, https://news.qq.com/a/20100203/001242_1.htm (in Chinese).

Yuan, Y., Wang, F.F., 2019. Blockchain—Theory and method. Tsinghua University Press, Beijing, China, 108–109 (in Chinese).

Zscheischler, J., Brunsch, R., Rogga, S., Scholz, R.W., 2022. Perceived risks and vulnerabilities of employing digitalization and digital data in agriculture—Socially robust orientations from a transdisciplinary process. *Journal of cleaner production*, 358, 132034.

Conclusion
Integration of Zhongyong and Digital Technology Has a Bright Prospect

At present, although agriculture, as a traditional industry, often takes a cautious attitude toward novel cutting-edge technologies, agricultural digitization is widely welcomed by the public (Pfeiffer et al., 2020). Besides, digitization is also expected to make a significant contribution to addressing several challenges facing agriculture, such as growing food demand and increasingly tight resource utilization (Annosi et al., 2020). This is also the crisis faced by global agriculture under the current situation of the COVID-19 epidemic. Under the acceleration of the agricultural digitization process, the connectivity between humans and technology in the agricultural value chain will continue to increase with the increase of transparency of agricultural practice, while the digitization of the agricultural system will challenge the balance between inherent agricultural stakeholders (Fielke et al., 2020). Therefore, for agriculture, under the surging trend of the digital wave, the most urgent demand is to conduct interdisciplinary governance research at the intersection of digital technology and agriculture, reduce the risks brought by the technological change to agriculture, and explore the digital agricultural framework and how this framework can support and reshape the traditional agricultural mode.

On the other hand, there are also many research studies on green data centers and blockchain in the field of agricultural digitalization. Most of the research on green data centers focuses on information security and server scheduling optimization, but some research involves agricultural digitalization. Momtazpour (2017) introduced a design-time technique for energy-efficient design of a green data center farm in Iran, due to the use of coordinate descent

DOI: 10.4324/9781003369660-7

to optimize the management system such that energy management in data centers can save an average of 11.6% of costs. Al-Zamil and Saudagar (2020) proposed an energy-efficient IT framework including green data centers for the agricultural sector in Saudi Arabia, which is committed to energy efficiency, low cost, and environmental friendliness. Ferrag et al. (2020) proposed a four-layer IoT-based green agricultural architecture that includes data centers and blockchains, which can save electricity to the greatest extent. Liu (2021) analyzed the problems existing in the intelligent marketing of agricultural products in the era of big data, and put forward suggestions for building a large data center for intelligent marketing of agricultural products.

In contrast, the theoretical and applied research of blockchain in agricultural digitalization is more abundant. Patil et al. (2018) proposed a smart agricultural communication framework based on the combination of IoT devices and blockchain, which can provide secure and lightweight communication services for smart green-house farms. Leduc et al. (2021) sorted out most of the existing blockchain-based agricultural frameworks and believed that most frameworks focus on food tracking and traceability, and pay little attention to digital market design, so they proposed a blockchain-based agricultural market platform. Dey and Shekhawat (2021) proposed a blockchain and IoT e-agriculture integration frame-work, which aims to improve the forward and backward linkages of the agricultural value chain, benefiting the participants in the value chain and enhancing the IoT network performance. Torky and Hassanein (2020) conducted a comprehensive survey on the importance of integrating blockchain and IoT in developing smart applications for precision agriculture, and proposed a blockchain model for IoT-based precision agriculture. The combination of the IoT and the blockchain can make the management mode of preci-sion agriculture more autonomous, effective, and intelligent. Iqbal and Butt (2020) proposed an agricultural blockchain model with a centralized farm management system as the blockchain node, which incorporates the repelling and notifying system based on the IoTs. It keeps crops safe from animals.

All in all, combing the existing research shows that most of the research involving technology integration and focusing on agricul-tural digitalization often combines data centers with the IoTs, or blockchain and the IoTs. There are few studies that integrate green data centers with the blockchain and use the Zhongyong philosophy to analyze the pros and cons.

On these grounds, we draw lessons from the Confucian Zhongyong thought in our research on the basis of analyzing the pervasiveness of green data center and blockchain. Based on the three necessary conditions of the Zhongyong practical method, we demonstrate the Zhongyong practicability of the combination of green data center and blockchain. Then, taking Beijing Liuminying Ecological Farm as an example, a semi-centralized and semi-decentralized circular agricultural framework is proposed. This framework integrates all the core technologies of green data center and blockchain and combines the two technologies to achieve the purpose of "complementary advantages, advantages restrain disadvantages, disadvantages offset disadvantages" so that green data center and blockchain as well as their inherent technical characters of centralization and decentralization are in a Zhongyong equilibrium and realize the Zhongyong combination. A series of opposite and dependent objects or concepts such as "centralization" and "decentralization", "high efficiency" and "low efficiency", "autocracy" and "democracy", "monopoly" and "sharing", "information island" and "openness", "high leadership" and "fragmentation of collective decision-making power and executive force" constitute the intersection of technological logic and philosophical logic. The intersection makes this circular agriculture framework based on green data center and blockchain conform to impartial "Zhongzheng", inclusive "Zhonghe", and the "Zhongdao" of fairness, justice, and science, which provides feasible reference scheme for the digital evolution and sustainable development of agricultural mode. However, there are some deficiencies in this study, which are worth thinking about and need to be further explored and improved in the future.

First, although the study draws lessons from the Confucian Zhongyong, and completes the theoretical analysis and proposes the physical technological framework from metaphysical concepts, and with specific cases, it still stays at the level of technical architecture. In the future, two technologies, green data center and blockchain, can be constructed in the integrated development platform of the green data center, Docker image of Bitcoin test network, Ethereum-decentralized app, and other blockchain application development platforms to conduct field test and inspection on the whole digital agricultural framework. Then the test and inspection results are fed back in real-time to further improve the technical details and refine the theoretical knowledge, and constantly revise the practical direction of agricultural digitization. It can also speed up the construction of the digital road of Beijing Liuminying Ecological Farm.

Second, Beijing Liuminying Ecological Farm is a specific case. In this study, the magnificent theory is concentrated on specific cases for framework building. This approach makes the research more vivid, substantial, and targeted, but the universality of the research needs further discussion. Although theoretically speaking, green data center and blockchain can be used for any digital transformation of agricultural scene or case, but the scheme of agricultural digital transformation is not unique. In addition to the current popular green data center and blockchain, big data, cloud computing, IoT, VR, digital twin, and other technologies also provide diversified technical solutions for the application development and mode transformation of agriculture. Even if the green data center and blockchain are also used, the details of the technical architecture are different due to the different practical problems faced by different agricultural scenarios. In the future, in addition to the Beijing Liuminying Ecological Farm mentioned in this study, more micro case studies can be carried out in other agricultural scenarios. In this way, more agricultural digital transformation schemes based on green data center and blockchain can be proposed, and the single case study can be expanded to multi-case study, and the case library can be enriched to enhance the validity of cases and the universality of technical solutions.

Third, with the vigorous development of digital technology, agricultural digitization has become one of the development modes of future agriculture, and sustainable agriculture represented by green agriculture, ecological agriculture, and circular agriculture is also one of the future agricultural development modes. There are differences in the goals and concepts of the two modes, and the emphasis is not the same. Will this difference have a collision in the specific practice? Can the relationship between "digitalization" and "sustainability" achieve a state of Zhongyong equilibrium? These questions are not discussed in this study. In the future, in addition to practical landing applications and vivid multi-case studies, more theoretical analysis and carding can be carried out at the macrosystem level. Through the combination of qualitative and quantitative research, we can further study the similarities and differences between agricultural digitization and sustainable agriculture in organizational management, production efficiency, technological innovation, environmental externalities, and other issues. On this basis, the philosophical logic contained in the Zhongyong is used to interpret it. The philosophical logic and technological logic are once again bravely "embraced". Through rigorous argumentation, induction, and summary, more thoughts and suggestions can be provided for the development of agriculture in the future.

References

Al-Zamil, A., Saudagar, A. K. J. 2020. Drivers and challenges of applying green computing for sustainable agriculture: A case study. *Sustainable Computing: Informatics and Systems*, 28, 100264.

Annosi, M.C., Brunetta, F., Capo, F., et al., 2020. Digitalization in the agri-food industry: The relationship between technology and sustainable development. *Management Decision*, DOI:10.1108/MD-09-2019-1328

Dey, K., Shekhawat, U. 2021. Blockchain for sustainable e-agriculture: Literature review, architecture for data management, and implications. *Journal of Cleaner Production*, 316, 128254.

Ferrag, M.A., Shu, L., Yang, X., et al., 2020. Security and privacy for green IOT-based agriculture: Review, blockchain solutions, and challenges. *IEEE Access* 8, 32031–32053.

Fielke, S., Taylor, B., Jakku, E., 2020. Digitalisation of agricultural knowledge and advice networks: A state-of-the-art review. *Agricultural Systems* 180, Article Number: 102763, DOI:10.1108/MD-09-2019-1328

Iqbal, R., Butt, T. A. 2020. Safe farming as a service of blockchain-based supply chain management for improved transparency. *Cluster Computing*, 23(3), 2139–2150.

Leduc, G., Kubler, S., Georges, J. P. 2021. Innovative blockchain-based farming marketplace and smart contract performance evaluation. *Journal of Cleaner Production*, 306. Article Number: 127055.

Liu, X. Y. 2021. Agricultural products intelligent marketing technology innovation in big data era. *Procedia Computer Science*, 183, 648–654.

Momtazpour, M. 2017. Towards designing a green data center farm for Internet services: Iran's case study. *The Journal of Supercomputing*, 73(4), 1600–1628.

Patil, A. S., Tama, B. A., Park, Y., et al. 2018. A framework for blockchain based secure smart green house farming. In International Conference on

Ubiquitous Information Technologies and Applications, International Conference on Computer Science and its Applications (pp. 1162–1167). Springer, Singapore.

Pfeiffer, J., Gabriel, A., Gandorfer, M., 2020. Understanding the Public Attitudinal Acceptance of Digital Farming Technologies: A Nationwide Survey in Germany. Agriculture and Human Values, DOI: 10.1007/ s10460-020-10145-2

Torky, M., Hassanein, A. E. 2020. Integrating blockchain and the internet of things in precision agriculture: Analysis, opportunities, and challenges. *Computers and Electronics in Agriculture*, 178, 105476.

Index

For Product Safety Concerns and Information please contact our EU
representative GPSR@taylorandfrancis.com
Taylor & Francis Verlag GmbH, Kaufingerstraße 24, 80331 München, Germany